Lest We Forget

Poems Of Peace

Edited By The Young Writers Team

First published in Great Britain in 2025 by:

Young Writers
Remus House
Coltsfoot Drive
Peterborough
PE2 9BF
Telephone: 01733 890066
Website: www.youngwriters.co.uk

All Rights Reserved
Book Design by Ashley Janson
© Copyright Contributors 2025
Softback ISBN 978-1-83685-401-2
Printed and bound in the UK by BookPrintingUK
Website: www.bookprintinguk.com
YB0636AZ

Foreword

Our latest poetry competition, *Lest We Forget*, focuses on war and the impact it has had throughout the years. We asked young poets to pen their thoughts on the subject, either reflecting on the horrors of war, the impact on those left behind, or a hope for resolution. With conflict still rife in the world today, it's a subject that cannot and should not be avoided. It's important to acknowledge the sacrifices, fear and pain that some people still have to face, and these young poets have done just that.

Some of the poetry in this collection focuses on the direct experiences of war: the sights, sounds, smells and emotions, creating a vivid picture in the mind's eye. Other poets explore the difficulties faced by those who are left behind, and the emotions of waiting for your loved ones to return, uncertain if they ever will.

Here at Young Writers our aim is to encourage creativity in children and to inspire a love of the written word, so it's great to get such an amazing response. The result is a collection of thoughtful and moving poems in a variety of poetic styles that also showcase their creativity and writing ability. Seeing their work in print will encourage them to keep writing as they grow and become our poets of tomorrow.

I'd like to congratulate all the young poets in this anthology. However they chose to express their thoughts and feelings, the resounding effect is a powerful one: a continuous battle for freedom, hope, and above all, a cry for peace.

Contents

Independent Entrants

Cheyanne-Louise Fury (11)   1

Coopersale Hall School, Epping

Amelia Green   3
Abigail Fleming (11)   4
Jack Tyson (12)   6

De Warenne Academy, Conisbrough

Leah Proudman (12)   7
Katie B (12)   8
Zuzia J   9
Chloe Farrar (14)   10
Ruby Louise Hughes (12)   11
Ameila C   12

Glyn School, Ewell

Joel Bongers (11)   13

Hungerhill School, Edenthorpe

Farrah Bingham (12)   14
Rosie Cresswell (11)   15

Kempston Academy, Kempston

Lianah Shaw (14)   16
Ryelan Minshull   18
Fraizer Bal (14)   19
Tanvir Basra (13)   20

Landau Forte Academy QEMS, Tamworth

Isla Clark (12)   21
Skye Hollyoake (12)   22
Kitty Fudge (12)   23
Henry Prosser (12)   24
Esmeralda Cooper-Percival   25
Peyton Neal (11)   26
Maksymilian Romaniuk (12)   27

Ontrack Education, Roundswell Business Park

Lex Jones (14)   28
Mitch Brooks (17)   29
Alexis Tuitt (15)   30
Sienna-May Casburn (14)   31
Zak Phillips (15)   32

Outwood Academy City Fields, Wakefield

Fatoumata Badjie (13)   33

Rooks Heath School, Harrow

Reshteen Sargand (17)   34
Aditya Sharma   36
Malak Roumieh (13)   37

Sir Henry Floyd Grammar School, Aylesbury

Isobel Sutherland (14)	38
Millie Holmes (14)	40
Amelie Glover (12)	42
Katharine Biddulph (14)	43
Holly Mayer (14)	44
Mathilde Phipps (11)	46
Elika Hares (14)	48
Lara Hunter (15)	49
Lily Bowler (11)	50

Soham Village College, Soham

Isidora Abbot (11)	51
Phil Collins (13)	52
Zoey Manning (11)	54

St Francis Of Assisi Catholic College, Aldridge

Annie Cartwright (11)	55
Emilia Skrzypczyk (12)	56
Carlo Notarantonio (13)	57
Blake Hunt (12)	58

The Adeyfield Academy, Longlands

Eshal Fraz (11)	59
Aaron Jenkins (15)	60
Marni Tranmer (11)	62
Alfie Smith (14)	64
Beatrice Gurney (13)	66
Angel Grevatt (13)	68
Tao Chiew (11)	70
Ayesha Butt (11)	72
Emily Garrity (13)	74
James Delderfield (11)	75
Ellen Timmis (14)	76
Samarveer Singh (12)	77
Owen Devine (14)	78
Jasmine Suleman (14)	80
Nikkia Cameron (13)	82

Aeryn Rogers (13)	84
Paige Evans (11)	85
Kyle Fogarty (12)	86
Harry Wells (13)	87
Harry Sims (14)	88
Sophia Jevon (12)	89
Imogen Randall (11)	90
Dylan Dalphinis (11)	91
William Kret (12)	92
Maram Oueslati (12)	93
Hope Roberts (13)	94
Josh Fredericks (14)	95
Alexsandrea Davies (14)	96
Mollie Stanbridge (11)	97
Nataliya Fulleylove (14)	98
Logan Clarke (13)	99
Rianna Cojocaru (12)	100
Alice Howes (13)	101
Ruby Balfour (12)	102
Jessica C (11)	103
Charlie Davis (13)	104
Matei Iancu (13)	105
James Johnson (14)	106
Toby Willson (13)	107
Iliuta-Madalin Fasui (12)	108
Iasmina Nicolaica (12)	109
Alfie Hammond	110
Bailey Jenkins (11)	111
Charles Demanya (13)	112
Amy Sheard (14)	113
Connie-Mae Walker (13)	114
Zayn Akram-White (11)	115
Mariana Mantuani Braganca (13)	116
Isadora Madelane (11)	117
Alfie Sturtivant (12)	118
Lexie Jones (12)	119
Tamsin Botha (13)	120
Lauren Deacon (13)	121
Taylan Osler (11)	122
Haydn Rutledge (11)	123
Jaziah Cameron (11)	124
Olivia Ellemore (12)	125
Evelyn-Rose Rogers (12)	126

Charisma Sibanda (13)	127	Lylah Akram-White (12)	170
Skyla Long (11)	128	Quinn Tucker (12)	171
Ruby Raffety (12)	129	Keira Merrick (12)	172
Max Ramsamy (13)	130	Edie Lowe (12)	173
Alfie Bleakley (14)	131	Nate Barringer (12)	174
Rachel Cooksey (12)	132	Yakira Peri-Taylor (12)	175
Harbour Edwards (11)	133	Jessica Speirs (14)	176
Kamila Zywina (14)	134	Mya Caseman (13)	177
Maisy Hart (11)	135	Florence Lilley (11)	178
Daria-Elena Pruteanu (12)	136	Michael Hitchman (11)	179
Anamaria Nozadze (11)	137	Alex Curtis-whittaker (11)	180
Rose Larkin (13)	138	Amber Wiley (13)	181
Sienna Howard (12)	139	Oliver Wharfe (11)	182
Ella Mutlu (12)	140	Ollie Jones (12)	183
Declan Hall (11)	141	Joshua Ball (12)	184
Rubie Tait (11)	142	Jessica Renyard (11)	185
Evie May (11)	143	Maddie Smith (13)	186
Adam Waller (12)	144	Sophia Ward (11)	187
Molly Canaj (11)	145	Edward Matei (12)	188
Darius Irimia (11)	146	Jessica Renyard (11)	189
Dulcie Bland (11)	147	Charlie Wharfe (14)	190
Oliver Cox (14)	148	Cassidy Farkas (12)	191
Grace Marshall (13)	149	Lucie Evans (13)	192
Jessica Murphy (14)	150	Riley Summerfield (11)	193
Alexander Pazhev (11)	151	Rahil Khan (11)	194
Julia Schmidt de Oliveira (11)	152	Lucas Butler (12)	195
Rocco Weatherley (12)	153	Oscar Harris (12)	196
Amelia Markland (11)	154	Mateo Jalba (12)	197
Michael Butterworth (12)	155	Malakai Hamidy (12)	198
Jaime Donnelly (12)	156	Abbas Juma (13)	199
Michael Ngoma (12)	157	Chloe Carter (13) & Ellie-Marie	200
Ellie Maidment (11)	158	Jack Gransden (12)	201
Khaira Joosub (12)	159	Evie Thomas (11)	202
Kaiden Gair (13)	160	Frankie Harthill (11)	203
Beau Zikmund (13)	161	Haris Khan (14)	204
Bobby Garrad (11)	162	Grace Wells (12)	205
Archie Howard (13)	163	Kaitlyn Johnson (11)	206
Logan Pope (12)	164	Katie Southam (13)	207
Alex Przybylski (12)	165	Lily-Grace Wingrove (14)	208
Lilly Juster (11)	166	Gurneet Kaur (11)	209
Obie Proctor Mckeown (11)	167	Hollie (11)	210
Drew Campbell (11)	168	Maryam Iqbal (11)	211
Summer Ford (14)	169		

The West Grantham CE Secondary Academy, Grantham

Lana Gidlow (12)   212
Hope Howkins (13)   213

Ysgol Gynradd Gymunedol Gymraeg Llantrisant, Miskin

Dylan Wilkins (10)   214

The Poems

What Could Have Happened If It Wasn't Like This?

For those who sacrificed to be known,
We should value to our bones,
As we remember those people for their actions,
Nothing will stop us from remembering you no matter what happens.

As new poppies grow,
We must be at peace with the ones who once had a glow,
As new soldiers come and go,
We must remember everybody has a low.

Children scream,
And all we can wish is that it was a dream,
Worry about family,
Is always a tragedy.

Being a target,
Never having enough to go to the market,
Hungry, starving,
Having to be slowly passing.

New life has come,
I start to numb,
I am never enough,
Nothing is helping it from being tough.

The courage soldiers have to move forward,
Oh how the death of thy soldiers not to be slaughtered,
Prayers of the town's people,
Oh how the rivals were evil.

Forever on you may rest,
You are all known for your best,
Forgiveness and peace,
Unlike your enemy evil and blue,
You are bright, shining, and true
From the world you tried to beat.

Cheyanne-Louise Fury (11)

Forced Where The Poppies Grow

Forced to fake their age,
Where the poppies grow.
Forced to fight for land,
Where the poppies grow.
Forced to sacrifice their life,
Where the poppies grow.
Forced to be separated from relatives,
Where the poppies grow.
Forced to shoot their friends for 'cowardice',
Where the poppies grow.
Forced to rebuild their life,
Where the poppies grow.
Forced to set off bombs,
Where the poppies grow.
Forced to let the horses die,
Where the poppies grow.
Forced to have a lingering of pain looking at memorials,
Where the poppies grow.
Forced to accept the fact more than sixty percent of soldiers and doctors have an unnamed grave,
Where the poppies grow.
Forced to keep going,
Where the poppies grow.

Amelia Green
Coopersale Hall School, Epping

Why Are The Poppies Red?

Why are the poppies red?
Does anyone know?
Although we won't be certain
We can guess what happened where the soldiers lay
Maybe it symbolises the blood
They're red like the blood
Blood from the wounds that gave the soldiers excruciating pain
Drip, drip of the blood giving the petal design
Drooping gently like the frowns found upon their faces
They hold up their weapons
And however fearful they are
They step forward and make history
So maybe the red is to symbolise courage
Determination, resilience, and commitment
Possibly it's a reminder
Of the time they joined for Christmas
Playing football in the snow
People sharing trenches with others
You know, though, that this didn't last
Maybe the red poppies show the significance of the festivity of the colour red
To remind us of the times when the soldiers had a break to celebrate
Just like we did

So a piece of us joined to them
By the white flakes that fell from the sky
On a day no one could forget
I know why the poppies are red
The poppies red for me
My great-grandfather
That was his favourite colour
Red.

Abigail Fleming (11)
Coopersale Hall School, Epping

Remembering The Soldiers

Remembering the soldiers who fought in the war
Thousands lost their lives to the cannon's roar
They defended our country and paid the supreme price
We are thankful and proud for their sacrifice
Red poppies are the flowers of peace and love
Remembering those soldiers in heaven above.

Jack Tyson (12)
Coopersale Hall School, Epping

Do You Remember?

Do you remember the soldiers who died in the war?
Do you remember how their flesh turned raw?
Do you remember how their bodies dropped to the floor?
And how their lives were torn?

Do you remember their children waiting for them to come back?
Do you remember how they were told to stop cutting slack?
Do you remember how they had to carry hundreds of bags?
Away from home, living in their rags?

Do you remember the trauma they had to endure?
How the soldiers never got to stay indoors?
Their lives they never got to explore?

Remember them, not just for one night
They died so you could live
November 11th, remember them.

Leah Proudman (12)
De Warenne Academy, Conisbrough

For Our Lives

For our lives, you live freely,
For our lives, the world is less scary.
For the Jews, for all the colours,
For the people who had to suffer.

We gave our lives for the world,
We gave our lives for history to unfurl.
Don't cry, don't fret,
You have so much more to live for yet.

Today is so much better,
Today you don't have to be a fretter.
Let this be our letter to the world.

"Yesterday," they cried,
And so many died.
And for those who did not survive,
To you we owe our lives.

Katie B (12)
De Warenne Academy, Conisbrough

Those Poppy Fields

Out there, those glorious poppy fields,
A sight called beautiful by all,
Out there, those glorious poppy fields,
Do you remember how many made their fall?

Out there, those glorious poppy fields,
Red like soldiers' blood,
Out there, those glorious poppy fields,
Stained red with death and tears that flood.

Do you remember, out on those glorious poppy fields,
How many men stood?

Those glorious poppy fields,
A memorial for all who fell,
Those glorious poppy fields,
Never forget what story they tell.

Zuzia J
De Warenne Academy, Conisbrough

War

People screaming, crying, fighting,
Artillery fire flies overhead, with the sound of bombs.
We don't know who will win,
But we know we'll lose loved ones.
What does it all mean, why war?
Is it the answer to peace?
No! Why would it be?
Young men are forced to join the army.
War means the country falling apart,
War isn't the answer.

Chloe Farrar (14)
De Warenne Academy, Conisbrough

Remember, Remember

R emember, remember
E veryone who fought in the
M ilitary during the wars, and
E veryone who believed and cheered them on
M embers who fought in the war, their
B odies gone from the face of the Earth
E veryone will remember them
R emember, remember.

Ruby Louise Hughes (12)
De Warenne Academy, Conisbrough

The 11th Of November

A day to remember
Was the 11th of November
The fields stained with blood
The 11th of November
Was indeed a day to remember
As the bloodshed finally paused
We should remember the 11th of November
And those who before it died
Never forget the 11th of November
Or those who died for this cause.

Ameila C
De Warenne Academy, Conisbrough

Dead Or Alive?

Why would you go to all the trouble of war?
When the first one saw enough of blood and gore,
When peace is gone and hopes are dwindling,
And you're searching for anything to use as kindling,
When the night is as cold as your enemy's hearts,
And you are wracked with pain and scars,
Settling down for a troubled night's sleep,
Hoping desperately that you'll get forty winks,
Without the gunshots and screams getting into your dreams,
And the sounds of your companions mumbling in their slumber,
Until your body succumbs to the darkness,
And the noise outside is quiet,
Not knowing if you'll wake up again,
Dead or alive?

Joel Bongers (11)
Glyn School, Ewell

Poppies And Memories

Poppies bloom down below, between the cross
Row on row.
When you think of the memories, we all share our future.
Remember them from the past.
Know they will be there when we are hurting and believe, be strong.
We shall not sleep.
We shall only remember.

Farrah Bingham (12)
Hungerhill School, Edenthorpe

For Those Who Have Fallen

Although we grow old,
The tower has still fallen.
Poppies still stand high around them,
Waving in the sky. Before they perished.
Loved ones fall,
Waving desperately for attention.
Hopefully, we will never see this day again.

Rosie Cresswell (11)
Hungerhill School, Edenthorpe

War And Peace Poem: In Our Memory

I stare out at the morning sky,
A fresh and precious poppy in my hand,
I watch an overhead robin fly,
I try to understand;
Will I be a memory in the future,
Like all the other strong soldiers that forged on before me?
Will I be of any use in the future?
Is my life and death, my fighting onwards, simply a story?
Will I just be a memory?
There is this flower in my hand,
This draught in the young, morning air and it beckons me.
I realise now that I am ready to fight,
That nothing bad can come of a loyalty so noble and so right.
I think of the trenches, the pain, the bullets raining down.
What happens if I survive the war? Will I be seen as some sort of hero when I get older?
All the stories I've been told of sobbing mothers and sons fighting,
Waist-deep in mud and filth. Metal hats reflecting shells and streaming tears.
Amputated limbs become missing parts of themselves.
That is all they are. A memory.

The poppy falls from my hand to the ground,
Grazing the grass as it does,
It is a feather landing safe and sound,
It is like a sign from above.
The flower stands for so much more than just bloodshed.

And now I realise it is about a community in familiar faces -
of soldiers who forge onwards beside me.
It is about sacrifice and glory,
In this dawn, and in this hope.
In our memory.

Lianah Shaw (14)
Kempston Academy, Kempston

Fields Of Red

In the quiet dawn of morning's light,
We gather hearts, both solemn and bright.
With poppies worn and heads held high,
We honour those who dared to try.

Through fields of red where courage lay,
Brave souls who fought, who paved the way.
Their whispered tales in the winds we hear,
A legacy cherished year by year.

Lest we forget, their sacrifice,
A promise made at such a price.
In shadows cast by battles bold,
Their stories of valour and hope unfold.

In 2024, we pause to recall,
The bravery, the duty, the love for all.
Their dreams now stitched in freedom's thread,
A tapestry woven by those who bled.

So let us stand with gratitude clear,
Remembering those we hold so dear.
With every heartbeat, every breath,
We honour them, lest we forget.

Ryelan Minshull
Kempston Academy, Kempston

Lest We Forget

Lest we forget, in silence deep,
The ones who gave us dreams to keep,
Who held the weight, who paid the cost,
In battles won, and lives lost.

Through muddy fields and smoky air,
They marched ahead, troubles shared,
With hearts of iron, yet soft with grace,
Each step they took in death's embrace.

Their stories woven into time,
Of a sacrifice, both harsh and kind,
They left their homes, their names unsaid,
To shield the vast future in their stead.

The poppies bloom where once they lay,
Bright petals speak what words can't say,
Yet they ask us not to glorify,
But hold their truth beneath the sky.

Lest we forget, our freedoms stand,
On gifts of courage, hand in hand,
A legacy we won't ever regret,
In whispered thanks, just in case we forget.

Fraizer Bal (14)
Kempston Academy, Kempston

Salute

Lest we forget, those are the words
Let the lost souls soar like birds
Leaving their swords, leaving their shields
On the dreaded battlefield
Let their memories
Be remembered for centuries
They may be weak or strong
But their influence will last long
They gave words to those who could not speak
Every person is unique
The soldiers' hearts are pure and minds are clear
They are the reason why we are here
We are in great debt
We will never forget
The sacrifices they made
And all of the aid
After the war's done
There's always a next one
But the heroes keep the fight
To save us, it's right.

Tanvir Basra (13)
Kempston Academy, Kempston

Lest We Forget

L et them rest in the field of poppies, the bold, the violent, the fallen.
E ven in the horrors of war, hope stands proud with unwavering nerve.
S till, the telegrams were distributed, sadness was spread like a virus.
T hey crumble to their knees, families grieve, brotherless, husbandless, fatherless.

W e will remember them: the ones who fought on the beaches of Normandy, the ones who flew like birds with
E verlasting memories of home etched in their minds, hoping to waltz with their wives once more.

F or they fell, they sense their loved one close by, waving them goodbye.
O ur troops tried to help but sometimes, it was too late. Tales of sacrifice forever told.
R un when the sirens sound, the bombs are on their way, to the station underground to hear a distant rumbling sound.
"G et down, bomb!" they bellowed, soldiers suffering, lives cut brutally short.
E ven though their lives were lost, they did it for us, for our future, for world peace.
T hey will be remembered, they will be honoured, they will never be forgotten for the freedom they fought so hard to protect - we will remember them.

Isla Clark (12)
Landau Forte Academy QEMS, Tamworth

His Memories Evergreen

It was finally Christmas Day
Yet something was amiss
A veil of sadness hung in the air
Adorned in nostalgia's kiss
In the warmth, the laughter seemed to fade
As whispers of worry cast a pall
Feeling lost, I sought refuge instead
I fled the chatter to the kitchen's glow
Where a letter lay in shadow's embrace
Unsealed and waiting, its secret to show
'Sent from Afghanistan', a haunting trace
That night, as I nestled in dreams so deep
A weight of sorrow pressed on my chest
When my mother entered, her tears made me weep
"I have something urgent, it's time I tell"
My heart plummeted as truth took its toll
The emblem of valour, the Warwickshire crest
In my mind, a soldier, a hero, a soul
Now I bear the weight of memories bittersweet
A legacy carved in love's endless song
Though he's gone, his courage doesn't retreat
In my heart, the bravest man will always belong
For my memories of my grandfather are evergreen.

Skye Hollyoake (12)
Landau Forte Academy QEMS, Tamworth

Family

People come and people go
Like river's endless gentle flow
Some are friends, some drift apart
Yet family stay close to heart

Through laughter and shadows deep
They hold our hands, our secrets keep
In every smile, in every tear
Their love surrounds us, always near

Though miles may stretch and years may fly
The ties that bind won't fade or die
For family is more than blood or name
It's warmth and strength, a steady flame

And when we're lost or feeling small
It's family who will catch our fall
In their embrace, we find our way
The ones who love us, come what may.

Kitty Fudge (12)
Landau Forte Academy QEMS, Tamworth

Poppies

With all the destruction, silence fell
Soldiers lying, many feeling unwell
Yet through all this destruction, a piece of hope shines through
Dozens of poppies growing out of the blue

Red poppies, the blood of the soldiers
Purple poppies, the animals that suffered through all the roller coasters
Black poppies, the unity of race
White poppies, innocent lives that cannot be replaced
All importantly, like the soldiers who fought
We remember them, without another thought

Now that it's over, healing takes place
Pink poppies like the newfound love: never being misplaced
Orange poppies, the symbol of healing
And yellow poppies, the ability to start a new self-healing.

Henry Prosser (12)
Landau Forte Academy QEMS, Tamworth

Those We Lost And To Those Who Came Back

The men who saved our country, many men,
Family stories left untold,
Only a few survived and came home to their family.
Yet some families lie there waiting for those who fought,
But never came back.
These men fought for our country and for a good deed,
However, so many lives were lost, families were devastated.
One thing we can do is respect, and give a minute
To those we lost and those who came back.
To honour their families and them.

Esmeralda Cooper-Percival
Landau Forte Academy QEMS, Tamworth

War Is War

Men fighting, risking their lives
Shooting, shouting, what is the price?
Bullets in hearts, shattered to parts
No hug goodbye, just hear them cry
Torturous nights, bed bug fights
No family home will be known
With fingers crossed, children are lost
No father known at home sweet home
Pools of tears, nightmare fears
Dying for them as the poppy grows by its stem
Love is love, home is home
War is war, where hearts are torn.

Peyton Neal (11)
Landau Forte Academy QEMS, Tamworth

Remember, Remember

Remember, remember
Those who have died
Fought for us
And never came back

The brave, the few
Who gave it their all
Who tried to save the world
For me and you

We pray for those who died for us
Showers of love we send to them
Thank you all
For what you've done
For we won't forget
The brave and strong.

Maksymilian Romaniuk (12)
Landau Forte Academy QEMS, Tamworth

The Pigeons

A flurry of flaps and into the blackened sky it has gone
Churned up and becomes distant, small
Rows of deep trenches appear as if they could be lines of ants

The scent of burning fuel cannot be escaped, even in the air
Like its wings, it is carried by the currents

Gunfire has quietened but the night is not still
Plane engines grumble, hungry for blood

The air is thick against the beating of its wings but no matter
It must continue onwards

Measly grains scattered across the dirt are little reward for the perilous flight but reward nonetheless

Again into the sky it rises, again the twine around its foot grips too tight
There are always more letters to carry
That is until there are not.

Lex Jones (14)
Ontrack Education, Roundswell Business Park

Never Forget

War looks like the face of a drained soldier, who has been fighting for his country and loved ones.
War smells damp of the wet uniforms of soldiers, crawling through wet mud, over the corpses and rotting flesh of their friends and enemies.
War sounds like the screams of the dying and the living, bangs of gunshots, booms of grenades, buzzing of aircraft and the cheers of our brave soldiers and their sacrifices.
War feels dark, lonely, and scary. When you are surrounded by others, you still feel alone.
War tastes bitter, sharp, and salty. The taste of mud, death, and salty tears lingering in your mouth.
War reminds me of hardship, the unwavering sacrifice of soldiers fighting for the freedom of everyone.
Lest we forget.

Mitch Brooks (17)
Ontrack Education, Roundswell Business Park

Scary

War looks scary like no scare has looked before. It looks like a nightmare you just can't escape from, a nightmare that will stay with you when it is over and you are awake.
War smells like broken trees, smoke from the guns that are shooting at the soldiers, bodies of the brave soldiers who lost their lives fighting for us and our country.
War sounds like scared soldiers running from the enemy, like the crying of families when they get that dreaded call.
War feels like a never-ending bad dream that you just can't quite get out of or wake up from.
War tastes like dust and nightmares and gravel and friends that you can not see ever again.
War reminds me of a dark time that I hope we never go through again.

Alexis Tuitt (15)
Ontrack Education, Roundswell Business Park

The War To Remember

The war looks like the world is ending and exploding,
The war smells of smoke and burning.
The war sounds of planes flying and dropping bombs,
The war tastes like rotten flesh.
The war feels cold like ice, scary as a clown and as dark as the night,
The war makes you feel lost and alone with nowhere to call home.
The war reminds me of the people who died to save our lives and our country,
Always remembered and never forgotten.

Sienna-May Casburn (14)
Ontrack Education, Roundswell Business Park

The Senses Of War

War looks dark and faded, like an empty Polaroid,
War smells sharp and hot, with sulphur glazing your nose,
War sounds silent, yet blazing, not all war was on the field,
War feels harsh, with pain past the point of imagination,
War tastes cold, runs dry and pitiful,
War reminds me of the endless struggles of others,
Lest we forget.

Zak Phillips (15)
Ontrack Education, Roundswell Business Park

In Fields Of Red

In fields where poppies gently sway,
We pause to honour, remember and pray.
For those who fought, for those who fell,
In battles fierce, where heroes dwell.

Their courage bold, their spirits high,
They faced the storm, they touched the sky.
With hearts of steel, nerves of fire,
They marched for peace, their one desire.

The silence now a solemn sound,
In memory of the battleground.
We wear the poppy, red and bright,
A symbol of their endless light.

So let us vow with voices clear,
To keep their legacy ever near.
In fields of red where poppies grow,
We honour those who faced the foe.

We will remember them.

Fatoumata Badjie (13)
Outwood Academy City Fields, Wakefield

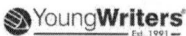

As It Is

All quiet up-front,
There - just there - with the wind flickering the thrush from the dance field.

Some 'foreign' field they claimed, 'forever England', though others fought on that dust.
Over a few minute bullets of honour their dignity damned lay,
Much ado of their march incited them to talk with arms upon thrust.
Many shock-shells ready to leak with unbranded wine gushing forth their crust
Exiting the purple pipelines off of hapless, hopeless, ceaseless souls at bay.

"Light up the canons and rifles marked reload,
Ignite the ventricles and atriums circulate!"
Ecstasy bolts their spirit nought failed nor bellowed,
Sparks catapult on all lest their oil be no more to find fate.

Fie o'er thy lofty palace walls! Upon debt art thou heavy:
Under each passing one 'crosses the barrier 'neath their muzzle -
Their mirrors of shattered chances. I would pray 'peace'
If the Keeper of Heaven cleft the doors, by even a bristle, for me.
Lo - even yet - and behold! They engrave the earth by their strife and struggle.

Ev'ry joint'd axis ought to reap their recompense after their toil.

Sorrow weighs on sorrow coated by a familiar grief scarf'd on regrets.
Lies of old and renewal of truths upon seventy-three-score add one hundred six of those you count fleeting day by day.
Ere the glamour o' day bear witness to the glory from valiance,
Elsewhere the quiet strikes the ears numb to the flutter; therefore, by the Deservéd One - One and Only -
Peace... until after a time...

Reshteen Sargand (17)
Rooks Heath School, Harrow

Silent Grave

I took an evening stroll,
among the rambling graves;
where you can almost feel the essence,
of all the restless souls.
Whatever place you chose to tread,
seems oddly preoccupied.
It's almost like,
You don't feel in your place.
Living mingling with the dead.
The atmosphere turns from tranquil to a restless air,
Which makes shivers go up your spine.
A nervousness rises rapidly in your nerves.
The wind howls through the trees.
Then the eerie chant of crickets.
Every voice of nature is warning you.
You soon go,
but the graves remain, now numb,
and all goes back to sleep.

Aditya Sharma
Rooks Heath School, Harrow

The Sadness Of War

T renches filled with screaming soldiers
H ungry orphans crying all day
E verybody's life is ruined

S cheming generals ready for battle
A ngry mothers protecting their children
D eath and death and death
N o happiness, no joy
E mpty hearts and traumatised faces
S adness, fear and grief
S uffering and pain

O ver the seas, peace is not seen
F amilies are separated and killed

W ars are not necessary
A nd peace is what we want
R eunited we must stand.

Malak Roumieh (13)
Rooks Heath School, Harrow

We Will Remember

I remember
My father's booming laugh,
The twinkle in his eyes
As he won the game once more.

I remember
My mother's foreign melancholy,
The glint of tears in her eyes
As my father walked out the door.

I remember
My father's steadfast promise,
The belief in his eyes
As he told me he would win me the war.

I remember
My mother's collapse,
The devastation in her eyes
As she read the letter from the corps.

I remember
My realisation of chaos,
The casualties of war memorialised in my eyes
As I lay my father to rest forevermore.

Lest We Forget - Poems Of Peace

I remember
My son's refusal to listen,
The fire in his eyes
As he marched out the door.

I remember
My anguish,
The death replayed in my son's eyes
As he stumbled back from the war.

I will remember
My son's collapse,
The devastation in his eyes
As he learned to live again.

He will remember
My loneliness,
The suffering reflected in his eyes
As he lives on.

His son will remember
A world shaped by war,
The destruction of all our lives,
As he learns to live for all of us.

Isobel Sutherland (14)
Sir Henry Floyd Grammar School, Aylesbury

In Fire, Flesh And Blood

Bang
an order
over the top and out into the open
they run with me slung on their back
there's nowhere to go but straight forward
careful to dart through the minefield of soldiers
fallen but not forgotten.

Bang, fire
a warning shot, or a deadly shot?
from a comrade, or an enemy?
into the sky, or into bone?
if anyone were to never leave
would they really be
fallen but not forgotten?

Bang, fire, flesh
an enemy's chest
crimson blooms, a toxic flower
they sway with glassy eyes
before slumping to the ground
fallen but not forgotten

Bang, fire, flesh, blood
I am dropped to the ground
chained to the back of a soldier
no longer am I silky black

I am stained with dirt and with blood
blood, blood, blood, blood, blood
of the fallen but not forgotten

Bang, fire, flesh, blood, flower
red paper pinned to a coat
names are etched into stone at a memorial
a village now stands where there was once a battlefield
and somewhere amongst the dirt and the earthworms
me
the weapon of the
fallen but not forgotten.

Millie Holmes (14)
Sir Henry Floyd Grammar School, Aylesbury

Soldier's Plight

The poppies shine, so red, like blood,
Among the soldiers fallen dead on the mud.
The warriors' efforts so noble and true,
In order to make this world better for you.

These soldiers were determined folk,
Whose courageous spirits never broke.
Yet they felt sadness and overwhelming fears,
As they fought for their lives with guns and spears.

These armies did not choose to war and fight,
They were condemned to their sorrowful plight.
Happiness playing truant since September forty-five,
Never knowing whether they or their families would survive.

Cleanliness was nonexistent and sleep was scarce,
Their armour filled with mud, burns and tears.
No books, sports, or even a game,
Instead of TV, they watched houses aflame.

Miles they trudged: on and on,
To fight and live in trenches where no human should belong.
And yet the poppies shine, so red, like love,
Among the soldiers who died in faith on the mud.

Amelie Glover (12)
Sir Henry Floyd Grammar School, Aylesbury

Those Left Behind

Bitter, resentful eyes,
Upon the countenance of his brother,
As he inspects where the dead soldier lies,
One man for another.

Tumultuous, saddening skies,
Swirl above the bland, nameless graves,
Over the despairing mother, who cries,
About the daughter she could not save.

A gaunt cat padding softly down the street,
Scruffy, skinny, unkempt and unclean,
Wondering if he'll have anything to eat,
Since his owner is nowhere to be seen.

The horrors of war, raging even after it's through,
Because you can lose the people you loved, the people you knew.

Katharine Biddulph (14)
Sir Henry Floyd Grammar School, Aylesbury

Butterfly

Gazing at the clouded skies
Blood and rain washed through my eyes
The longing for home, a butterfly
Drifting closer, flying high

I'd left my home, my son, my wife
And decided to go and live this life
The panic of losing, a burning knife
A secret longing for the afterlife

But what was I thinking, I needed to go
Through this pain, through this woe
To see my family before I go
Standing, swaying to and fro

I was here for my nation, for my country
I was here for everything but me
I was here so that they could finally see
That in my heart I was free

But I didn't feel free at all
I felt so lonely, so scared, so small
The looming future, a towering wall
As the bullet sank, I fell, fell, fell

One last look at the clouded skies
One last tear seeped through my eyes
Dead on the ground, the butterfly
I clutched it tight, closing one last eye
Flying, flying oh so high.

Holly Mayer (14)
Sir Henry Floyd Grammar School, Aylesbury

Humans Just Won't Change

What happened to the world
When the guns started firing
The tanks started rolling
The people started shouting

Why didn't we think
About who we were shooting
Or the people we were killing
People
People

Families
Friends
Girls and boys
We were turning on each other
Human to human

Not once did we think
Or talk it out
Not once did we stop
To realise

So why do we fight?
Why do we kill one another?
Why do we bother when life matters so much more?

Because people don't think
And they don't talk it out
Or stop
Or realise the horror that they started
It's not that people won't change
It's that they don't want to.

Mathilde Phipps (11)
Sir Henry Floyd Grammar School, Aylesbury

Family Of Fallen

She sits and thinks of her father
A man sent off to war
A man sent back, broken and battered
Not able to walk once more

She wobbles when she thinks of her mother
A woman who took to the sea
A woman who witnessed the horrors of man
Her mind full of things most beastly

She weeps when she mourns her brother
A young man proud to serve
A young man proud to protect his brothers
His death one that shall unnerve

She lies and cries in her room
A family taken by war
A family taken by the horrors of man
A part of them that's hard to ignore.

Elika Hares (14)
Sir Henry Floyd Grammar School, Aylesbury

A Little Alive

I drink my morning whiskey, my heart beats, a little more alive.
I greet some others in the dirt and rats, on my way to get my weapons, on my way to fight.
I make my way to the others, time to cross the top, my heart beats.
I take my gun, begin to cross the top, fire and blood.
I hear it and see it, they fall, my heart breaks.
I feel a pain in my neck, a bullet wound, I fall.

I watch them drink their tear-dropped whisky, their hearts wrench.
We are remembered, a little alive.

Lara Hunter (15)
Sir Henry Floyd Grammar School, Aylesbury

Remember Them

In Flanders fields, the poppies grow,
By the graves, in beautiful rows,
People flow in, to pay their respects,
For those whose lives were sadly wrecked,
By the cruel war where they served their countries,
And, despite our pleas,
They could not be saved,
As what they braved,
Was far too much to bear,
And they could no longer breathe air,
Fallen, lost, but never forgotten.

Lily Bowler (11)
Sir Henry Floyd Grammar School, Aylesbury

Remember

R ationing, their tummies growled, empty and dark
E choes of hopeless cries deaden the gentle whispers of the night
M umbles of the fallen in hospital bays
E mbers of fires crawled through the streets of London
M emories of loved ones are all we have left
B loody faces bruised with terror
E mpathy we give to those affected
R emember those lost, never forget.

Isidora Abbot (11)
Soham Village College, Soham

No Victory Is A Win

No victory is a win
No surrender is a loss
No hatred is justified
No win is a true win because

Soldiers are condemned by promises of glory
The gunshots that boom
The dying that scream
Binding them to a fading tomb

So long ago, hatred was a plague
Though, it's spread even more today
Remembering them, that is our mission
As without them, our world today would fade

Planes overhead, thundering along
Their pilots, knowing there would be no return
A job they signed up for to defend their country
Would lead to their impending doom

We have all the reasons to remember them
All the reasons to never forget
All the reasons to praise them in silence
All the reasons to remember the loss

So stand with me, in silence
So stand with me, to remember
Stand with me to remember their suffering
Stand with me to remember, their final fight, their last win, the eleventh of November.

No victory is a true win
No surrender is a loss
No hatred can be justified
No win is a win because of their symbol, their cross.

Flowers bloom on wasted fields
Poppies bloom on their footprints
These flowers that bloom on a home of death
These flowers are how we remember.
Silence. Poppies. Remember.
The last surrender, the eleventh of November.

Phil Collins (13)
Soham Village College, Soham

Lest We Forget

All I can see is soot and ash,
People falling down in a flash,
Wounds of battle cover my face,
What led me to this horrid place?

Friends and family all at home,
Everyone squashed in a small dome,
Children taken onto a rickety track,
Will their mum or dad come back?

Zoey Manning (11)
Soham Village College, Soham

Off The Boats!

6th June 1944, I will never forget.
Sitting in the boat, my mind was racing with the thought of the onset.
The call was raised, "Off the boats, Off the boats!"
A prayer to the Lord, and a lump in my throat.
Please, Lord, keep me safe.
We run like a herd of animals into the dark, dank, cold water.
I feel protected in my pack, for now. My mind's eye sees the smile of my only daughter.
This vision will keep me safe.
As I ran, I heard the battle cry of the aeroplanes above. So, so loud!
Ready for battle, weaving in and out of the dark clouds.
Extra forces to help keep us safe.
I join in with 10,000 men's roar of war.
Heavy, cold and wet, we reach the shore.
I see the enemy, run and charge, dear Lord, keep us safe.
A bloody battle ensued that lasted twenty-four hours.
Blood, death and sadness to regain power.
My fellow men and I, joined in a common mission, we fought to keep each other safe.
The battle ended but the war was ongoing.
We had done our job today, but the sadness in our hearts and the emotion on our faces was showing.
Britain, today, we kept you safe.

Annie Cartwright (11)
St Francis Of Assisi Catholic College, Aldridge

Untitled

June 6th, 1944
Troops rushed in the morning,
Soldiers fell, crashing to the ground,
Trembling, the others ran,
The tension was unimaginable.

Troops rushed in the afternoon,
Men of all ages fought,
There was no retreat,
There were endless attacks until their last second.

Troops rushed in the evening,
Bullets flying through the sky,
They'd pray to be safe,
Or to have no life, to be away from their suffering.

Troops rushed in the night,
For twenty-four hours, there was no stop,
The pain and agony these men went through,
For we hope that their torture will be forever over.

Emilia Skrzypczyk (12)
St Francis Of Assisi Catholic College, Aldridge

D-Day

The boats set sail at morning light,
Soldiers ready for the fight.
On Normandy's shore, they made their way,
For freedom's cause, they would not sway.

The waves were cold, the sky was grey,
But they were brave on that fateful day.
Through crashing bombs and bullets' flight,
They pressed ahead, hearts filled with might.

The beaches echoed with battle's roar,
Yet still they pushed, from sea to shore.
With every step, with every breath,
They faced the danger, defied the death.

Now we remember what they gave,
The courage shown, the lives they saved.
On D-Day's shore, so far away,
They fought for peace we have today.

Carlo Notarantonio (13)
St Francis Of Assisi Catholic College, Aldridge

D-Day Poem

On distant shores, where waves once roared,
Our soldiers stood, with hearts that soared.
Eighty years have come and gone,
Yet still their courage goes on.

Through stormy seas and skies of rain,
They fought for freedom on that day.
Each step they took, each breath they gave,
Made freedom's path, for us they saved.

Time may fade, their greatness remains,
A testament to freedom's gain.
Within our hearts, their memory fast,
Forever strong, it ever lasts.

Blake Hunt (12)
St Francis Of Assisi Catholic College, Aldridge

The Price Of Peace

In Flanders fields, the poppies grow,
Each one growing row by row,
In remembrance of the dear soldiers buried down below,
They fought for our days, they fought for our life,
They gave all they had to endure the strife,

Innocent children torn from homes they knew,
While others found new dreams to pursue,
They whispered of peace in a world full of fear,
While longing for parents who never drew near,

Young men forced to fight,
With hearts full of fear but minds set alight,
Brave soldiers praying for peace,
Yet the war rages, their hopes still increase,

Across the seas, the cries were heard,
As hearts broke in silence, without a word,
A soldier's sacrifice, a family's pain,
Their love remains, but loss will reign,

Now we stand, their legacy to keep,
Their courage sown in hearts so deep,
Through every tear, their strength we find,
A lasting love through hearts combined,
In Flanders fields, the poppies blow,
A symbol of love where we too grow.

Eshal Fraz (11)
The Adeyfield Academy, Longlands

Underneath Shadows, Hope Flickers (Lost Within)

In the depths of a shelter, I wander alone,
A prisoner of war, with no place to call home.
The echoes of gunfire, the scent of smoke and fear,
Haunt me still, as I search for a way to persevere.

The walls are cold, the darkness is vast,
I stumble and fall, with each step I take at last.
The memories of loved ones, lost in the fray,
Torment me still, as I try to find my way.

The sound of bombs, and the screams of the slain,
Ring in my ears, like a haunting refrain.
I am lost, with no direction to follow,
A leaf blown by winds, with no place to hollow.

In this labyrinth of concrete and steel,
I search for a glimmer, a light to reveal
A way out of this darkness, a path to the sun.
But it's hard to find when the heart is undone.

The weight of the world, the burden of pain,
Crushes me down, like a mountain's heavy rain.
I am but a shadow, of a man I once knew,
A ghost of a soul, lost in a world anew.

Lest We Forget - Poems Of Peace

But still, I hold on, to the hope in my heart,
A flame that flickers, a light that will not depart.
For in the darkness, there is still a spark,
A glimmer of courage, that guides me through the dark.

I rise up, with a newfound might,
And face the unknown, with a warrior's light.
I push through the rubble, climb through the pain,
And emerge into the sunlight, with a heart that's not in vain.

For though I am scarred, though I am worn,
I am still alive, and my spirit is reborn.
I have faced the horrors, of war and its might,
And emerged stronger, with a heart that's still alight.

So let this be a lesson, to all who can see,
That even in darkness, there is still a way to be free.
For in the depths of a shelter, where I once was lost,
I found a way out, and a heart that was not the cost.

Aaron Jenkins (15)
The Adeyfield Academy, Longlands

Why Have War?

I have slumped down so many nights,
These past six months hard to write.
As I look around my heart sinks,
And eyes fill with cries.

I crave peace but dwell on anger,
My mind and spirit are at war.
War must stay out of here,
Peace must linger here.
Why make shooting sounds?
Why not stay safe and sound?

I often wonder about life,
About family, parents and my future wife.
You stand in a trench sinking with mud,
And the bitter cold wind freezes your blood.
We know it's all fake,
We know it's for no sake,
We know there is an end,
But our egos won't mend.

They were the dead,
Short days ago,
The feeling of dread,
And the sky's filled with red.

I won't play tug o' war,
I'd rather play hug o' war,
Where we hug,
Instead of tug.
Where everyone giggles,
And rolls in the rug.

I knew a simple boy,
Who grinned at life in empty joy,
Slept soundly through the lonesome dark,
And whistled early with the lark.

Soldiers were average men,
Who did courageous acts.
The river's a hoarder,
And he buries down deep,
Those little treasures,
That he wants to keep.

Life can seem ungrateful and not always kind,
Life can pull heartstrings and play with your mind,
I'll keep a little tavern,
Below the hill's crest,
Wherein all grey-eyed people,
May set them to rest.

Marni Tranmer (11)
The Adeyfield Academy, Longlands

Lying Causes Crying

Word has spread,
The war has begun,
We must fight, they said,
Or else we'll be shunned.
Lying causes crying.

We hear a knock,
We open the door,
Only a peep,
I can't stay anymore.
Lying causes crying.

We were told we'd be safe,
Fighting for our country,
Our victory great,
All needed is entry.
Lying causes crying.

They lied to us,
They lied about intentions,
Now we are just dust,
Our names are unmentioned.
Lying causes crying.

We fought the same as others,
Maybe even better,
But we are looked down upon,

Like some type of critter.
Lying causes crying.

Our bodies lie here,
Silent and pale,
This isn't some fiction,
A movie, or a tale.
Lying causes crying.

We miss our family,
They miss us too,
Don't ever forget,
What they made us do.
Lying causes crying.

Now please remember us,
For we gave you life.
We aren't very known,
Our names etched in stone.
Lying causes crying.

Now no one cries,
Despite all the lies,
Despite all the trying,
Lying causes crying.

Alfie Smith (14)
The Adeyfield Academy, Longlands

The Poppy Of Ensuing Sorrow

My eyes shoot open
Body trembling as I jolt upwards
The familiar sound of gunshots
Absent from the field
Fearing the worst
I scramble to the front lines
It is quiet, too quiet.
Peering over the edge of the trench
Eyes widened with terror

Blood, blood everywhere
Corpses litter the land
I tremble with fright
Our leaders cheer with delight
"We won! *We won!*" they cried

We... won?
We... won?!
I turn to tell my closest companion
Only to see him dead in a ditch
It all comes crashing down

No, no
This can't be real
He can't be dead
Right...?
I kneel beside his lifeless form
Hands shaking in their gloves
I pull his war-torn corpse
Into my warm arms

Pearly tears stain his reddened uniform
From among his rotting flesh
A plant begins to sprout
Petals as red as the blood spilt
It sprouts upwards
Its bud unfurling
Into a beautiful
Beautiful poppy

Poppies sprouted from all those lost

Young or old
Ally or axis
Despite our differences, all were humans
Why must we fight...?
Why...

Do innocent people have to die?

Beatrice Gurney (13)
The Adeyfield Academy, Longlands

The Lies That Took Lives

Manipulated, gaslighted. Innocence stripped away,
Just a game? Just a bit of friendly amusement?
Until you get in that trench and lie is excoriated,
A lie that made many die,
A lie that left people's heads in a mess for life,
A lie that soon became a force,
Not a choice.

Blood of innocence leaks out. What for?
Was it a game to play with your mates?
Yet you're the only one left in the end.
You see them go up to the skies,
Leave you behind knowing that you're next,
Because of the innocence that made you believe it was just a game,
But it was all covered by a picture-perfect frame,
A frame that hid the veracity,
A frame that told you anything but the truth,
Lies, lies, lies.
Now you've got nothing but the sound of cries.

Blood runs like a river through the dugout homes,
You're left in the darkness, the hope is lost,
You have nothing left as all is gone,

Lest We Forget - Poems Of Peace

Stabbing shots fly through the air,
One bullet will eradicate a life,
And if you are one to survive,

You're left with screams running through your mind.

Angel Grevatt (13)
The Adeyfield Academy, Longlands

From War To Rising Hope

From sins of sorrow to valleys of hope,
Cries of forgiveness echo whilst trying to cope.
Empty souls wander around,
Seeking love in a childhood town.
In tombs of joy but sadness too,
The smell of fumes reminds the cold bombs.
Eating away at the bloody platforms,
Yet courage and hope still appear.
"Never give up!" they say,
But still remains the sense of fear.
Bloodlust, greed and murderous intent,
Global wars across day and night.
Light guiding the way all through the fight!
From the distance sounds of swords clash away,
Wars amongst the valleys of pain.
As fate spins, a thread without end,
New life draws its first breath.
On that day, all peace broke away,
While in hiding and bawling folk.
Held on to the last piece of hope,
Silence grew in the spaces between.
Violence started to end,
Rising up, as a chorus of souls find a voice.

Flickering through the void, these little sparks cling onto light,
Everyone is caught in this struggle.
And when the storms of change fan the flames,
Scattering ashes to tomorrow!

Tao Chiew (11)
The Adeyfield Academy, Longlands

Lest We Forget

Something I could hear
I could hear soldiers screaming and shouting.
I could hear bombs bombing and guns shouting
Bang! Bang!
Everything I could hear now was nothing like what I wanted to hear.

Something I could smell or taste
I could smell and taste the terrible tinned rations.
I could also smell the gas coming from the bomb.
Everything I could smell now was nothing like I wanted to smell.

Something I could see
I could see my courageous companions falling to the ground.
I could see the gory, gross blood all over the floor.
Everything I could see was nothing like what I wanted to see.

Something I could touch
I could touch the heavy guns and the weighty weapons.
I could feel the dirty, smelly clothes rubbing against my body.
Everything I could touch now was nothing like I wanted to touch.

Something I could see in a year's time.
I could see myself with my family and the world at peace.
I could see myself and my fabulous family eating something tasty.
Now that was what I wanted.

Ayesha Butt (11)
The Adeyfield Academy, Longlands

Courage

So much respect for those who lost their lives
"So much courage; they're so brave!"
And yet it often feels like people spit on their graves
Despite the sacrifices of the past, people have happily forced all of us to dive.

Do you think they *wanted* this?
Do you think they wanted to put their lives on hold for some petty leaders' cause?
Wouldn't it have been better if they never fought at all?
Maybe, alongside remembrance, we should focus on prevention so we don't have to do what they did and can keep living in ignorant bliss.

Yet some still push for war
Leaders and blind followers discriminate and fight, hoping for escalation
They want there to be *more* tension in their nation
They want there to be fighting and death and make sure no one's different anymore.

Is *this* what they wanted all their courage to go towards?

Emily Garrity (13)
The Adeyfield Academy, Longlands

A Lullaby For The Fallen

The sun was setting over the fields, painting the sky in soft shades of gold and rose.
The battlefield, once scarred and torn by the fury of war, was now still.
The ground was quiet, the only sound was the soft rustling of leaves in the wind, the distant hum of a bird singing its evening song.
Private James Telford sat on the edge of a trench, his rifle by his side, remembering all the fallen comrades.
His uniform was dirty, his boots worn down from weeks of marching, but for now, there was no fighting. No cries of battle. Only the profound, almost unnatural silence.
The others, his fellow soldiers, had gone to rest, lying down among the fallen, their faces peaceful in their stillness. Some of them had passed during the battle, others were lost in the chaos. Telford could hear their names in the quiet, a soft whisper that seemed to come from the earth itself. The war was over for them.
For everyone here.

James Delderfield (11)
The Adeyfield Academy, Longlands

Remember Them

It was not so long ago,
Those at the age of eighteen fought and so,
We remember them with poppies held close to our hearts,
And send love to those who may be falling apart,
War is not for the weak,
Those who tiptoe in the trenches to seek,
If they falter it is their graveyard they will lie upon,
We will cry for peace, shouting in unison.

It was those to fight what they ponder,
Not allowing a single thought to wander,
Who fulfilled their jobs in the war,
To save our country, name, and much more,
Now give us peace and let us rest,
We grieve again for you killed my loved one when they were fighting their best.
At what worth is the cost of someone's life
When it makes those around them feel as if they are being stabbed by a knife?
They left their all on the battlefield,
Your love will always be their strongest shield,
Remember them.

Ellen Timmis (14)
The Adeyfield Academy, Longlands

The Tragedy Of War

War is a time of tragedy
Soldiers fight in a battle for their country
Lives are lost and souls are shattered
Until one remains victorious
People die due to the destruction of war
Children evacuate to stay safe
Soldiers were brave
They risked their lives so they could protect their country
Why war, why not peace?
We can't enjoy freedom if war is going on all the time
Remembrance Day is an opportunity
To remember those who died in war
Why is war even a thing?
Can we just live in a world with peace and harmony
Faces were covered in blood
Fields are drenched in mud
Gunshots can be heard
People scream over someone they know lying dead on the floor
Buildings destroyed and countries deceased
Once standing long ago
I think war is unacceptable
Unfortunately, it still continues today.

Samarveer Singh (12)
The Adeyfield Academy, Longlands

On My Way

I'm on my way
To the battleground
Where I will most likely lie
I'm on my way
To the war.

I'm on my way
To possible death
Time to take my final breaths
I'm on my way
To the frontline.

I'm on my way
To the battle
Where we are just cattle
I'm on my way
To the trenches.

I'm on my way
To the trenches
Where the stench fills the
Air with pollution
I'm on my way
To the Germans.

I'm on my way
Never going home
We sit here all alone
I'm on my way
To the grave.

I'm no longer on my way
I've arrived at my destination
Fighting for this glorious nation
The trench is cold and wet.

But there is no time to be upset
When there is constant fire
I wish I was on my way home.

Owen Devine (14)
The Adeyfield Academy, Longlands

The Red

Blades of sage glass penetrated
Our bodies while we lay conscious
Left astray
For what was stained on that glass?
Red

We fought our battles
Even if yours shall continue
Yet what is it we shed?
Red

Her dress, her lipstick, her heels
She that I left to heal the plague of our sins
Red

The flash of godly light with the cracks, the crashes
The revolting clanks which we heard just before seeing
Red

He took us home, comfort in red was never what we sought
We would carry on the plague you summoned
The plague that was your sins
The same that was red

However, my heart that did shed, stained onto sage
Stabbed by the crash
The pain of which I felt
It was my love that remained red

It was the flowers that blossomed on the sage glass
That were red.

Jasmine Suleman (14)
The Adeyfield Academy, Longlands

What Is War?

What is war?
Is it a game,
Where people continuously risk their lives to win?
Where people play all their pawns until they all get knocked down?

What is war?
Is it a safe place,
Where soldiers are countlessly being hurt, killed and injured?
Where families at home are worried about them?

What is war?
Is it pressure,
Where soldiers stay constantly alert for sudden bombs or threats?
Where they have many restless nights thinking about saving their country?

What is war?
Is it hope,
Where innocent children hoping and praying for peace?
Where terrified parents are hoping for their children to come back to them?

What is war?
Is it justice,
Where the government decides what happens to the country?
Where the government decides who goes to war?

War is an unfair game.

Nikkia Cameron (13)
The Adeyfield Academy, Longlands

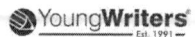

Don't Forget Like The Rest

The idea of war is glamourised too much,
Youth consider it fun to play games as such,
If they were exposed to what my men and women were,
I do tell you their vision would begin to blur,
Tears would trickle down their cheeks,
They'd be too traumatised to dare speak.

It pains to see the next generation act in such ways,
They enjoy battling each other in their video games,
While the people who gave their tomorrow for our today remain in the ground,
Hidden and locked away.

For only two minutes, we sacrifice our sound,
While others feel they need two months to say,
We deserve appreciation; they call out loud,
While our soldiers are beginning to be forgotten,
While their bones and flesh become rotten.

We don't appreciate them enough,
That's why war is glamorised too much.

Aeryn Rogers (13)
The Adeyfield Academy, Longlands

Lest We Forget - Poems Of Peace

The Adeyfield Remembrance Day

On the eleventh of November, I walk into school
As I look around I notice that there are students dressed in all types of uniforms
There are scouts, cadets, and plenty more.

In form time the head of house parades around collecting donations for the poppy appeal
Around the school I am blinded by the red sea of poppies decorating the hallways and classrooms.

In the second period the bell alarms ten minutes early
Everyone, students, staff and even Teddy, our school dog, rushes to gather at the courts
At exactly eleven o'clock, the Adeyfield Academy falls silent for two minutes
While we are paying our respects, our caretaker plays the trumpet.

The whistle blows to signal the end of the silence
Although the silence ends, our thoughts remain with those we lost
Lest we forget.

Paige Evans (11)
The Adeyfield Academy, Longlands

Endure

Awaken, ponder if we'll sleep at night.
Ration meals, bloody hands.
Guilt and dread perceive us.
Prepare to be sent out, one last wave.

Rounds of bullets penetrate the sky.
Dawn turns to dusk as we hide in the scarp.
Invade their territory, bullets fire, thrash their skulls.
Numbing weather, holding on.
Gain our strength through tears and pain.

Endure the weather, endure the wounds,
Endure the reality of this never-ending doom.
Wonder if we'll see our homes again,
Our families again, our neighbours again.

Once joy fulfils us, gloom represents us in the present.
Nazis invade, invade our lives, invade our homes.
Invade a once-powerful nation.
Endure this suffering, if it ever ends.
Lest we die, lest our nation be overcome.

Kyle Fogarty (12)
The Adeyfield Academy, Longlands

Poem About Sadness

War is rough and bloody
With people killing each other and so many lives lost
Just because people are risking their lives
For their country and their family

People are dying
Risking life for their family and their own life
So today we will remember the people who fought in WWI and WWII
And today we will come together to celebrate people's lives we have lost during the war

This is why we remember people who fought in the World Wars today
And the people who tried to save as many lives during the war
But they could not save as many as they wanted

Today we'll have two minutes' silence to remember people who died and risked their lives
And that is why we lay a wreath at the church
To remember people who died during the wars.

Harry Wells (13)
The Adeyfield Academy, Longlands

Remembrance Day

The day you remember
The day you pay your respects
You feel sorrow for people who have lost
You feel compassion for those who left and didn't come back
Never forget

The RAF protects us from the air
The Army protects our land
The Navy protects our seas and coasts
We remember those who fought
We remember those who served

We give our support to those who lost someone important
Our courage
Our compassion
This day we celebrate the victories and losses
So stand together and give your respect

When the clock hits eleven, stand silent for two minutes
To truly give your respect
Wear a poppy, the flower that grew on the battleground
Donate to help people in need
Help these people rest in peace.

Harry Sims (14)
The Adeyfield Academy, Longlands

Dover's Cliffs

Dover's cliffs are crumbling
Crumbling to their core
This is what will happen if you don't end the war
People will be different
Nature will change
And right before you know, life will never be the same

Dover's cliffs are crumbling
Slowly as I soar
Soar across the sea to slowly get to shore
To all women and children
Snuggled up in bed
Enjoy tonight and rest your weary heads
For men are out there fighting
Fighting for their lives
So you can have a future brighter than the sky

Now the war is over
Dover's cliffs are dead
Trees are bare
And fields are black
And everything is red
Red for all the blood
Red for all regret
Red for poppies growing fields where men rest.

Sophia Jevon (12)
The Adeyfield Academy, Longlands

Hard Times Are Worse But Going Home Is Better

I can see dirt on the ground and above me
I have to be aware of bombs and gas
And as I sit here today, I remind myself my family is okay
I sit here and say, "I wish I could have stayed"

Now, as I pray to the universe, I'm in my own little world
One of my troops awakens me as the gas enters
We run for our lives as we are saved
Gunshots in the background, lives being lost
As our friends and families lose their lives

We need to save our country
Then we can all go home if we survive
Medics, people screaming
Screaming in pain

I get shot but I'm not down yet
A medic saves me
It's 11/11 but I survived
I see my sisters, my family, my friends
As I run to hug them, we go home.

Imogen Randall (11)
The Adeyfield Academy, Longlands

Lest We Forget - Poems Of Peace

Was It Worth It?

As I look down at everyone from heaven
I can see everyone in silence for me
I lost friends and family
Family and friends lost me

I thank everyone for remembering me
In this beautiful country
In the minute of silence
Poppies are worn as soldiers are thanked
And I am one of them
That are thanked
Everyone is grateful
For the sacrifice I took

Even I am grateful for my fellow soldiers
Risking their lives beside me
But was it worth dying?
I could have been here with family and friends
But no, instead I sacrificed my life
To save yours
Was that the right decision?
I'm afraid I'll never know

I guess I will see you
In heaven, my friends.

Dylan Dalphinis (11)
The Adeyfield Academy, Longlands

End Of A War

The armistice created,
With hope for succession.
The end of the war, still awaited,
Soldiers, filled with depression.
While their countries are invaded,
They apply fierce and strong aggression.
Countries, still aided,
People, being taught misconceptions.

As the final shots are fired,
Battles nearing the end.
Soldiers, too tired,
Must still defend.
As they look at the fields,
They see a poppy.
They feel as if they are healed,
And although they feel sloppy.
The depression in their heads, cleaned.

Their general informed,
The soldiers greatly performed.
So as the lives they lost were mourned,
The First World War, deformed.

William Kret (12)
The Adeyfield Academy, Longlands

My Dream

I had a dream one very night that woke me up extremely late
The dream was that the Nazis got me, it filled me with hate.
I was screaming, crying, pleading that they would let me go
But they shook their heads, laughing and would always say no.

I remember the days when I took peace for granted
A time when bomb raids wouldn't happen and I wouldn't be killed with acid.
I crossed my fingers praying that someone would save me
But then the door broke down and men with guns and tin hats came out, I screamed, "It was the navy!"

I thank the soldiers, the lovely soldiers who sacrificed their lives
Who had to leave their beautiful children and their beautiful wives.

Maram Oueslati (12)
The Adeyfield Academy, Longlands

Every Time

Every time I wake up I lie there taking it all in
I am grateful that I live in the world I am in
Yes, there is war but we have people to fight for us
And because of that, I am forever grateful
Every time I wake up I am scared
Scared that one day I won't wake up
Scared that war will one day punish me and my family
Every time I wake up I am worried for the world
There is so much evil surrounding us and we don't even notice
Every time I eat I am sick to my stomach
Sick because I am so anxious about what's going to happen
To me, my family, my friends
I am scared
And there's nothing I can do to prevent it

All I can do is wait.

Hope Roberts (13)
The Adeyfield Academy, Longlands

The Sacrifice

The lives that were lost
The pain that I felt from the first shot
I may have saved others but at what cost?

Medics rushed over as I was on the brink of death
I didn't know what to do
I felt the cold air as I took my last breath.

My life flashed before my eyes
I knew that my time in war was over
I heard lots of screams and cries.

As they took me back to the trenches, I thought the worst
They covered my wound in bandages, knowing that I might not make it
I knew that my time had been served.

As I drifted away
I felt the warmth of other soldiers' hugs
I wish that I could still be with you today.

Josh Fredericks (14)
The Adeyfield Academy, Longlands

When I'm Home

Seeing the dirty rats brush
against my shoes,
smelling burnt wood on my
clothes was normal.
Hearing bombs go off every
minute was scary.
Touching the mud before climbing
up to fight.

Seeing my friends lying down injured
made me as cold as ice.
The taste of rice still makes
me hungry every time I talk.

In a year's time
I will be seeing my loved ones.
Finally, I'll be able to
taste my mum's roast dinner again.
Waiting to hear kids
laugh and play like chickens.
And I'll be able to hold
my wife and kid's hands again.

Alexsandrea Davies (14)
The Adeyfield Academy, Longlands

A Soldier's Story

I fought for my country,
I fought in war and I always knew it was forevermore.
My family was poor but no fear,
We had each other very near.
The red is blood and the black is whole,
And there I was as dark as coal.
There was one shot then three shots,
"I'm strong, I'm strong,"
I repeated to myself but I knew I was wrong.
I felt it coming but it was too late,
I feared that was my true fate.
I did it for my country, I'm proud I did,
But now I wish I would have hidden.
Now they raise a flag for us,
I was a good soldier, and they gained my trust.

Mollie Stanbridge (11)
The Adeyfield Academy, Longlands

Remember The 11th Of November

Remember me, although I have to say goodbye.
Remember me, I fought for this country,
I fought for our freedom
So, all I ask is for you to remember me.
Gather all your friends
And tell the story of World War One.
And when it ends,
Stand in silence for two minutes
To show your respect.
Remember all the fallen people.
Remember me, although I have to say goodbye.
Remember me, show your respect as the clock strikes 11am
On the 11th of November.
Wear a poppy on your chest as a sign of respect.
Remember me, remember the fallen,
Even if we have to say goodbye.

Nataliya Fulleylove (14)
The Adeyfield Academy, Longlands

The War

I woke from my sleep to the smell of gunpowder
I grabbed my gun and went out to my post
Then I saw an artillery shell land around the corner.

The taste of dirt hit me as the corner exploded, sending dirt everywhere
The gunfire stopped, and I got on rations of mashed potatoes
I started eating them with a spoon.

The gunfire continued, I went out to my post
The tower next to me fell down like a tree
I fell down, blinded by the dust.

I got up and wiped my face
I shot at the enemy
I had ham for dinner
I went to sleep at the end of the day.

Logan Clarke (13)
The Adeyfield Academy, Longlands

The Serving Soldiers

The serving soldiers
We will always remember
They were brave in war
Standing tall.

God was crying
As soldiers trampled through the mud
As explosions followed explosions
In the quest for peace.

As the rain fell from the sky
So did the planes
And soldiers fell onto their knees
Fighting for their families and their countries.

We will always remember the soldiers that we lost during war
We will remember where they fell
We will remember their courage
We will remember their sacrifices that they made
We will remember.

Rianna Cojocaru (12)
The Adeyfield Academy, Longlands

For Our Country

Every day I think of them, my wonderful family.
Every night I miss them, I write to them when I can.
But do they receive them?
I pray every day to make it out alive
To see my beautiful children and wife.
I want to save this country.
I want to do it for the soldiers who didn't make it.
Every morning I hear planes and bombs. It is scary.
Every afternoon I eat food made for animals.
To save our country
We sacrifice our lives.
For our country
We move away.
To help our country
To live peaceful lives again.
Lest we forget.

Alice Howes (13)
The Adeyfield Academy, Longlands

The Sadness Of War

He closes his eyes and rests his head,
For the war is over yet his friends lie dead,
The day of remembrance is sad and sorrowful,
Try hard to keep hope and don't let go,
Now take a deep breath and try not to weep,
For that time is over, you may now sleep,
The sound of gunshots hurts his ears,
It makes him feel like he has no tears,
I must warn you, the memories won't leave,
But the pain and suffering will,
For the future generations, he has great concern,
They must not let the world fall like the soldiers who did that day.

Ruby Balfour (12)
The Adeyfield Academy, Longlands

The Brave Soldier

I woke up in the morning with sweat hanging from my distressed face.
It was the day that I had to say goodbye to my family.
I was getting on my heavy uniform, trying to prevent it from flopping my back backwards.
I shed some tears.
But I knew I had to do it for my precious family... my country.
By the time I got downstairs, my back went numb.
And there they were, my family by the door, crying.
It was hard to see them cry.
My beloved children wouldn't let my arms go, nor would my dearest wife.
But I knew it would end soon...
I hope.

Jessica C (11)
The Adeyfield Academy, Longlands

Lest We Forget

L ife is lost during the sorrow,
E veryone is trying to survive.
S ome blaring sirens on the morrow,
T hen the soldiers begin to strive.

W hen the alarms blare, they start,
E very fight brings out the brave hearts.

F estivity for the heroes is not enough,
O r else history will be tough.
R egretting their choices seems right,
G oing to volunteer for the fight.
E very day we need to remember,
T hat's why we celebrate - 11th of November.

Charlie Davis (13)
The Adeyfield Academy, Longlands

When I Am At War

I can see my mates eating beside me
I can smell the flavourless porridge as I dig in with my spoon
I can hear some chatter and gunfire in the distance
I can feel the lukewarm billy can on my cold fingers

I can see an artillery shell go off far, far away
I can smell the blood in the mud
I can hear gunfire and grenades
I can feel the scratches on my gunstock

I will see my family in a year's time
I will hear the children playing outside
I will smell the roast dinner on the table
I will feel my children and my wife in a year's time.

Matei Iancu (13)
The Adeyfield Academy, Longlands

No Escape

Great Britain needed soldiers to fight in the war; they couldn't lose, not now, not ever.

The government thought and thought.

They found an idea, they posted it on paper and put it on walls, encouraging kids to join with the so-called fun.

The kids signed up thinking it would be an experience to remember and some kind of game, but they realised there was no escape.

Reality snapped, and worse came to worse.

Those young boys, husbands, dads, brothers, uncles, friends, lay there with no thought, dead for king and for country.

Lest we forget.

James Johnson (14)
The Adeyfield Academy, Longlands

Waves Of War

Over the top we go,
One after the other,
We're all mowed down.
And now we lie motionless in fields upon fields,
Flowers flourish upon our remains as it is a new time not to be disturbed,
Now we haunt the people who made us in this state.

To live in this everlasting pain,
To mourn over our empty graves,
That's where our bodies lie,
But our souls, they are free,
To roam the place that we once lived and see our loved ones for the last time.
We are at peace now in our tiny homes,
As we are the dead.

Toby Willson (13)
The Adeyfield Academy, Longlands

War

Wake up in the cold mornings,
Eat baked beans and potatoes,
Sleep if we could,
And fight for our country,
That's the thing we did for six years,
Or until we were brutally murdered by our enemies!
But at least we are remembered, right?
Now our families are safe because of us,
And you don't have to live in fear!
Will I ever be forgiven by the people I killed?
My kids waiting for me to come back home,
But I never returned,
The pain of not having a dad at a very young age.
We died to save the world.

Iliuta-Madalin Fasui (12)
The Adeyfield Academy, Longlands

Whispers Of The Fallen

The roar of the guns, the drumbeat deep,
When silence once would softly creep,
Now shattered by cries of men,
Fallen dreams in the dirt again.

In Flanders fields, poppies grow,
Next to the crosses, they row,
They mark our place, within the sky,
The cries above, singing by.

The earth is scratched,
In the trenches, the souls are sold,
For promises that cannot be told.

Children's hope filled the sky,
Replacing laughs with cries,
The aeroplanes align,
Near a fractured sign.

Iasmina Nicolaica (12)
The Adeyfield Academy, Longlands

Field Of Flowers

Fighting for their lives, wanting to go home,
But staying for their country because they know,
That if they gave up now, their family would be gone,
So they had to make sure every fight was won.
Their mothers worrying for them but could not control,
The fact that some of their sons may never grow old,
Peace was at last, though many fell,
And poppies began to grow,
Where others had gone down and now people know.
Why we remember the soldiers using poppies,
And why we have a minute to respect and to mourn.

Alfie Hammond
The Adeyfield Academy, Longlands

The Soldiers

In our country a few years ago
The war was concluded and we let poppies grow
The bombs that were dropped down from the sky
Caused our soldiers to be hurt and fly high

The heroes' families were in a horrible state
Yet they still died at a rapid rate
The two-minute silence we will perform
For our courageous men in uniform

Although the fight was extremely slow
We managed to succeed and beat the foe
We wear our poppies to remember
Our country's courageous and heroic helpers.

Bailey Jenkins (11)
The Adeyfield Academy, Longlands

My First Time At War

I can see me and my mates eating breakfast at war
I can taste the sweetness of my porridge
I can hear the tanks shooting
I can touch my billy can

An hour before, I saw soldiers shooting at each other
I could smell the gunpowder
I could hear guns firing
I was holding my gun ready to shoot

In years past, I could hear my children playing peacefully
I could smell roast chicken and taste apple juice
I could hear my children singing and laughing
I could touch my children and wife.

Charles Demanya (13)
The Adeyfield Academy, Longlands

Brainwashed

I stand in the icy trench, shoulder-to-shoulder
It is cramped and dirty, but at least we are somewhat safe
Hot gunshots and imploding bombs threaten us from above
Friends shout and scream moments before their bodies
come to a scarring stop
My body is fueled by fear and slop
We did not sign up for this
They said it would be fun
I have not written to my family in weeks
Too scared to tell them the truth
So instead I just count the sleeps
Until I either return home
Or die in this pit of lies.

Amy Sheard (14)
The Adeyfield Academy, Longlands

Thomas' Story

I knew a boy who lived for adventure.
Took every risk and every venture.
Littered with scratches and bruises in his youth.
But simply wanted to stay away from home in truth.
In vicious trenches, depressed and downcast.
Gunshots sent reminders of his past.
He flew a bullet through his heart.
And from the world, his soul did part.
During parades and moments of silence.
I can remember our gentle alliance.
And when the heartless jokes begin.
Rushing comes memories of his cold, wilted skin.

Connie-Mae Walker (13)
The Adeyfield Academy, Longlands

Remembrance Day

In the bitter cold of the morning, it was another normal day for Adolf Hitler,
All he had in his mind was being the richest man by invading countries,
So he invaded Poland,
But that made the politics of Great Britain radio him to say they would declare war with him if he didn't meet with them,
However, Hitler ignored them,
So England allied with France to fight the Wehrmacht,
USA and the Soviet Union later joined, which was the key to success.
So much suffering and pain for the cruel ideas of one man.

Zayn Akram-White (11)
The Adeyfield Academy, Longlands

Untitled

In fields green, and skies so blue,
A soldier stands, brave and true,
He answers the call, with courage bright,
To protect the day, and guard the night.

Through winds that howl and skies that weep,
He guards the land while others sleep,
For peace he fights, through battles roar,
To end the pain and stop the war.

The day will come when peace is near,
No more the sounds of cries and fear,
And in his heart, he'll always know,
That love and peace will help us grow.

Mariana Mantuani Braganca (13)
The Adeyfield Academy, Longlands

Poppy Fields

Now we lie in Flanders fields,
Full of all our lives and their lives upon the poppies,
The bright red of poppies shining all their might,
People looking down from the paradise,
Smiling with pride on their faces.

All of the mighty soldiers who fought for our lives,
With soldiers with hearts full of love and life,
They were brave to fight with all their might they had,
To protect us from World War One to World War Two,
And wearing poppies to commemorate those who lost their lives.

Isadora Madelane (11)
The Adeyfield Academy, Longlands

Hope

Trumpets play all through the day gone by
Hope stands as long as we try
It stands in the flags we fly
And the soldiers that fight
Hope seems far for those who have died
But hope still carries on for those in life
The poppies we wear that we buy
We buy them not to cry
But to think of those left to lie
The two minutes we look to the sky
To remember those who gave us hope in those times
Those who died
Being wished back alive
For the hope of us getting to say goodbye.

Alfie Sturtivant (12)
The Adeyfield Academy, Longlands

Remember The Past

The wind howls and my face turns to a frown,
As I remember the past.
People that aged,
And others who didn't age at all.
Help from others like washing hair,
And others we will never hear from again.

Remember the past,
As it's all gone too fast.
Dead or not,
Don't worry if you got shot.

Poppies are worn in memory of you,
As your intentions were true.
I'll keep your memory inside my head,
As I remember the past and you all who are dead.

Lexie Jones (12)
The Adeyfield Academy, Longlands

After He Died

Dead, died, tried
Wasted time, wasted life
He lies cold, still in strife
Shot by the enemy, healed by a friend
He killed himself in the end
Dead, died, tried

Brother, son, husband
Fought for his family
They look for clarity
Loved ones cry, little ones perplexed
Trying not to get vexed
Brother, son, husband

Gone, forgotten, buried
Stand in silence
After their violence
Remember the lost
After they were cost
Gone, forgotten, buried.

Tamsin Botha (13)
The Adeyfield Academy, Longlands

War To Peace

W ar hurts many but can save countries,
A ll soldiers leave home to fight.
R esults in tears and what normally is a crime.

T he families sit at home, waiting for the horror to end,
O nly to wait years, for their heart to mend.

P eople flee cities and towns,
E nd up in the countryside with a new mum.
A nimals get left in barns and pens,
C arry what you can but don't wait,
E verything could stop, and it has.

Lauren Deacon (13)
The Adeyfield Academy, Longlands

Some Time Later

As I woke up to the sound of gunfire
I see the enemy troops have started their advance towards the front line
As they rip apart our defence
Many lives are lost
We try to fight back
But the enemy artillery
And constant pressure
Is too much and quickly all goes black...
Sometime later
And a poppy field starts to show
Over the once barren and destroyed battlegrounds
Now these poppies show as a reminder
Of those who fought for our freedom
And did not make it back...

Taylan Osler (11)
The Adeyfield Academy, Longlands

On The Battlefield

On the battlefield, men had died.
Some peacefully while closing their eyes.
And others bravely, protecting the prize.
A fact that is known but should be said,
Is the men who died had been loved.
Let these words be spread.

In November, peace was declared,
As flags were raised and the good news shared.
As the news spread across the land,
People came together hand in hand.
As we stood together side by side,
Not forgetting the ones who died,
On the battlefield.

Haydn Rutledge (11)
The Adeyfield Academy, Longlands

Lest We Forget

There in a muddy trench eating food,
They could smell dirt and the smell of disease,
There had been terrible smells everywhere in the trench.
You could hear the sound of gunfire, tanks moving,
Shouting and talking everywhere.
They were in the muddy dirt,
All over the place,
As the French town was disgusting,
As a toilet would be today.
You could smell gas, poison, burning smells from the gun.
Also, there are the sounds of tanks' tracks,
And then there was war.

Jaziah Cameron (11)
The Adeyfield Academy, Longlands

Those Whose Lives Were Lost...

The battle scene was harsh.
The scent of blood erupted,
From the scattered, lifeless bodies on the ground.
Piercing and killing lives,
Noises of gunfire in my eardrums,
I want this war to end.

Why war, why not peace?
Why not stay gentle?
Why make shooting sounds?
Why not stay safe and sound?

My heart goes out to those who suffered,
Whether they came home,
Or lost their lives.
All should be remembered,
And all should be respected.

Olivia Ellemore (12)
The Adeyfield Academy, Longlands

Poppies Lie In The Fields

Copies of poppies lie in the fields,
Over and over all of the hills.
Planks of wood teamed together equal the cross,
To represent people in our loss.
The poppies are red like our fallen friends' blood,
Who now lie in peace under the memorial mud.
Why did this happen? "Who knows?" he said,
The one who knew lay down their head.
As long as we respect the remembered dead,
For now, poppies lie in fields,
Telling us a remembered story.

Evelyn-Rose Rogers (12)
The Adeyfield Academy, Longlands

Save The War, Save Us

This is a game not,
For why should it be as such?
When they sit and rot,
Because they know as much.
That's what they want you to know,
And so you do so.
That we are saving the show,
But you control the tempo.
This is a game not,
But the one functioning in our brains.
We can tie the knot,
And prevent this oh-so-gruesome blaze.
You can juggle this conflict,
Propaganda may not stand in your way.
I am passing this verdict.

Charisma Sibanda (13)
The Adeyfield Academy, Longlands

War

War was once here
1914 (World War I), which is 110 years ago
1936 (World War II), which is eighty-eight years ago
Years ago, war started, planes flying through the air dropping bombs
One after the other
My hands cramping when designing plans
One thousand drawings done in a day
Day by day
Month by month
Year by year
I will always be with you no matter what
Always looking down on you
My granddaughter
My everything
Love you.

Skyla Long (11)
The Adeyfield Academy, Longlands

Lest We Forget

Poppies glow as they grow,
Telling a story everyone should know,
Of brave men when they died,
So they could save many lives.

They had to sleep in deadly trenches,
Which were as hard as wooden benches,
Swaying softly in the wind,
Poppies remember the awful din.

As we remember the soldiers who fought,
We need to have lots of respectful thoughts,
For all the families who lost loved ones,
Due to the enemy's awful guns.

Ruby Raffety (12)
The Adeyfield Academy, Longlands

Innocent Individuals

Eyes too young to know such pain,
See the world in broken chains.
The skies once blue now burn with rage,
As innocence is caged in a war-torn age.

The cradle rocks in the quiet gloom,
A mother's tear, a child's doom.
Their future stolen, their hearts unsung,
For the wars of men, their songs are wrung.

But even in the darkest hour,
A child's spirit holds a flower.
Though war may steal, and death may claim,
In the ashes, hope still burns its flame.

Max Ramsamy (13)
The Adeyfield Academy, Longlands

A Line Of Soldiers

I can see a soldier on my right and left
The smell of dirt pollutes the air
The sound of guns echoes the trench
The feeling of hot food warms us
An hour before my friend lay unresponsive
An hour ago the smell of rot
An hour ago the screams like kettles
An hour ago the feeling of a dirty gun
In a year I see hope
In a year I will smell the fresh air
In a year I will hear the laughs of my kids
In a year I will feel my bed.

Alfie Bleakley (14)
The Adeyfield Academy, Longlands

The Day We Remember

We stand withdrawn, heads sunk low,
Remembering soldiers and those we owe.
Their courage lives on, even though they are gone.
A flame still flickers as the candle continues to burn on.
We remember, admire, and will never forget
The people who fought for our country without regret.
We pause today, with passion and grace,
Reminiscing all wounded souls, fallen and grazed.
Their sacrifice is eternal.
The years will not condemn.

Rachel Cooksey (12)
The Adeyfield Academy, Longlands

Loss Of Life

Loss of life,
Grief and strife,
War and violence,
Now just silence,
We fight no more,
There are bodies lying on the floor,
And as you lie on the floor,
Your heart slows its pound,
Your back feels wet,

You know you are hurt,
You are paying off your debt,
As your life seeps into the ground,
You fought to save people's lives,
But could not save yours,
We pray for you deeply and forevermore.

Harbour Edwards (11)
The Adeyfield Academy, Longlands

War

They remained still on the ground.
Charging forward,
They reached the other side.
Desperately clutch onto the fate,
Came our city's army.
But they are brave enough to protect the country,
Good or bad, they intertwine.
Clangs of swords, soldiers fighting,
Soon, dust settles on the battleground,
Bodies of loved ones are soon found.
In grief, we weep,
Thousands of good souls lost,
Simply tossed away.

Kamila Zywina (14)
The Adeyfield Academy, Longlands

I Might Not Be Around For Long

"I might not be around for long," he said,
I will try my best to stay strong,
I will fight at night,
And till dawn arises,
I will fight for others,
And I will fight for our peace,

As the silence crept in,
"There's only a few," he said,
I don't think I'll make it,
I don't think I'll make it till the next sunrise,
"I might not be around for long," he said.

Maisy Hart (11)
The Adeyfield Academy, Longlands

Echoes Of Silence

Echoes of silence, a soldier's lament
Bombs falling, men dying
Families fleeing and death rising
But what is the point of this war?
Why not have peace?
Why not have a world full of joy?
A place where life increases
Never decreasing
But what is the point of this war?
Men give away their lives
Their existence now hidden
Heads spinning
Death flooding your brain
What is the point of this war?

Daria-Elena Pruteanu (12)
The Adeyfield Academy, Longlands

The Haven And Soldiers

The haven is sombre there,
But we don't know where, when God will see
What we are doing, how will they feel, when they will
See how we are learning, then will they feel good? They did

Then something that made us live and they later made
S, O, L, D, I, E, R, S... and that makes soldiers
And we cannot forget how lots of people died for us
And always we can't forget what they have gone through for us.

Anamaria Nozadze (11)
The Adeyfield Academy, Longlands

Remember, Remember

Remember, remember,
The soldiers who died,
The soldiers who died for our lives,
The soldiers who died for our rights,
And the soldiers who died for us.

Remember, remember,
The struggling families,
Who worried every night,
Who wrote letters to their loved ones,
And didn't know if they'd make it back alive.

So, next time you stand in silence,
On the eleventh of November.

Rose Larkin (13)
The Adeyfield Academy, Longlands

Lest We Forget - Poems Of Peace

Keep The Faith

Oh! You who sleep in Flanders fields,
Sleep sweet - to rise anew,
We caught the torch you threw,
And holding high, we keep the faith,
With all who died.

We cherish, too, the poppy red,
That grows on fields where valour led,
It seems to signal to the skies,
That blood of heroes never dies,
But lends a lustre to the red,
Of the flower that blooms above the dead,
In Flanders fields.

Sienna Howard (12)
The Adeyfield Academy, Longlands

Pure Innocence

The wholesome children who didn't have a clue about what they were going through,
A heroic soldier's heart being torn apart,
The warriors with sharpened blades,
They shall be honoured in parades.

The trembling hands yelling in fear as the end was near,
The weaknesses that were in their eyes,
Were about to die,
From the pain and gain,
Oh, how they will be heroes yet again.

Ella Mutlu (12)
The Adeyfield Academy, Longlands

Lest We Forget

When I was in the war,
I was really tired of fighting,
So the leader told us we could have a nice dinner.
So we rushed to have some food,
And got right back to the battle.

I saw lots of planes flying above,
Rumbling the side of the trenches.
I heard lots of things like planes and even tanks,
Blowing the trenches up trying to win the war,
So I helped my team and fought.

Declan Hall (11)
The Adeyfield Academy, Longlands

The Warriors

There are three men sitting in the trench,
Pow! Pow! Pow! Pow!
Guns shooting behind them every second,
They have to beware otherwise they will get shot in the head.
Three men sitting in the trench eating what might be their last meal,
Which tastes like sardines.
Grenades going off on the other side of the team,
And just wondering whether they get to see their loved ones again.

Rubie Tait (11)
The Adeyfield Academy, Longlands

Soldiers Of The War

Hundreds of thousands of soldiers,
Running between boulders.
Risking their life,
Hoping to come back to their wife.
Praying to God they'll survive,
Thinking after this they could thrive.
Shot dead on the ground.
Some are found,
Some are left behind.
But it's good that we can remind them,
That they can be remembered.

Evie May (11)
The Adeyfield Academy, Longlands

Grenade

Grenade
War
Death
And Blood
Dead bodies in a flood
All covered in deep mud
This is death and murder
Done expertly like a hunter
They were taken like a burglar
During the cold, cold winter
This has made lives shatter
And where blood splatters
Where the poppies matter
And neither life nor death
Will ever matter
War, death
Grenade.

Adam Waller (12)
The Adeyfield Academy, Longlands

I Am Grateful

The life I have I am very grateful for
I am grateful that I'm not in danger
I am grateful that I'm protected
I am grateful I'm able to find food and water
Unlike others who had to survive in pain.

Tears come to my eye
When I think of war and soldiers who have passed
Today, 11.11.24, we respect people who fought
And it took place to save our country.

Molly Canaj (11)
The Adeyfield Academy, Longlands

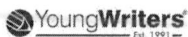

Lest We Forget

Rats squeaking and running across the trenches,
The smell of tears,
The power of bullets.
There's no one filled with glee,
Everyone in battle,
Gunshots getting fired,
People on the ground,
Everyone is tired.
Blood everywhere,
Everyone is freezing,
They're our heroes,
They're our saviour,
They do everything to keep our country safe.

Darius Irimia (11)
The Adeyfield Academy, Longlands

Remember, Remember The 11th Of November

Soldiers lie happy and proud
Some missing the people they lost
Children sing as it is all done
But never knew they wouldn't come back
Crying, weeping, standing up straight
As we remember what's good and what's great
Poppies growing on fields above
When people fought for us
Now we all stand up tall and free
Remember, remember the 11th of November.

Dulcie Bland (11)
The Adeyfield Academy, Longlands

The Other War

I wonder, when we think of them,
Do we really know who fought?
They did everything for our glory,
But we will never know their story.
Most of the soldiers died,
But the rest sat and cried.
And there goes all the time,
While other countries commit crimes.
When the sun goes up,
And the sun comes down,
All they were doing was
Fighting for the crown.

Oliver Cox (14)
The Adeyfield Academy, Longlands

Falls Silent

Everyone falls silent
It all started when they yelled fire
Poppies all around
And for two minutes, not a sound
Everyone appreciates you
Many miss you
When the night falls quiet
I think of you in that riot
As your spirit is so high
It always makes me cry
I will miss you, how you've died
And I'll look up to you, now you're in the sky.

Grace Marshall (13)
The Adeyfield Academy, Longlands

Flowered

Mud squelching beneath their boots,
Men fall.
They land with the poppies, the red pooling around, sharp pricking in the head.
The grass.
The sun is beautiful through their blurred eyes,
Explosions of yellows overhead.
They are alone, left behind.
The flowers will accept him, one of them he will become.
He will spend his days from here
Resting in the sun.

Jessica Murphy (14)
The Adeyfield Academy, Longlands

To The Great

I stand facing towards the cenotaph and I wonder,
Would they be proud?
Everything they fought for, would it be worth it?
Poppies red, glistening in the sun,
A reminder to us that they are the reason we are here.
It shows how much they fought and how hard they fought.
After all of that, they restored peace but not for long.
War reminds us of how they fought for us.

Alexander Pazhev (11)
The Adeyfield Academy, Longlands

A Field Of Crosses

Loss of love
Growth of grief
The ones who fought
Now buried deep
Stained by blood
The poppies grow
In a field of crosses
A war begins, a war ends
Though some are joyous
Others pretend
Don't forget the ones they have lost
Thank them for the freedom they have caused
The poppies grow
In a field of crosses placed row by row.

Julia Schmidt de Oliveira (11)
The Adeyfield Academy, Longlands

Darkness Of War

The darkness of war as dark as night,
Yet the poppies shine bright,
In line of death row,
Shadows of planes cover the bright light,
As they fight for our lives,
We pray for their life, hoping for just one more night.

Poppies rise, standing tall in the night,
They put their lives on the line for their loved ones,
Once gone but never forgotten.

Rocco Weatherley (12)
The Adeyfield Academy, Longlands

Lest We Forget

On the day the 11th of November
We remember the courage of soldiers who gave their lives
The memory of those happy days before the war
Remembering hope which they had once before.

Soldiers dripping in blood whilst stuck in the mud
Red flowers with seeds inside
Which prompt younger voices to ask questions swept aside
Gentle elders answer in pride.

Amelia Markland (11)
The Adeyfield Academy, Longlands

The Pain Of War

People fought to die
They tried and tried
But in the end, they fell.
Some survived, some aren't well
But in the end, we remember them
And all they did to protect us then.
We won't forget those brilliant men
And we will commemorate them
For all to see.
The poppy will be
On our chest, it will lie
To remember, commemorate thee.

Michael Butterworth (12)
The Adeyfield Academy, Longlands

Why Do We Remember War?

It goes silent
Why do we go silent?
Poppies are being worn
Why are many poppies being worn?
All you can hear are the crows
Why can you hear the crows?
The trumpet starts
Why do we remember when the trumpet starts?
People remember
Why don't more people remember?
People are sad and respectful
Why are they so sad and respectful?

Jaime Donnelly (12)
The Adeyfield Academy, Longlands

The Honourable War

To all the soldiers in war, I just want to say a good job,
Because you fought for our country, you are
War warriors in war.
Every night and every day,
All the struggle that you have faced, is now washed
Upon your resistance from the armed conflict today.
So, we honour you with pride because you're so kind, for
Ending this dreadful war tonight.

Michael Ngoma (12)
The Adeyfield Academy, Longlands

The Two-Minute Silence

The two-minute silence for the dead
I thought of the fields, when the fields were red
Red not with poppies, but with blood
The blood of men, the image of God
Two-minute silence for the dead.

Then stood in the crowd and bowed my head
Not in reverence but in shame
At the insight and memory of their name
Two-minute silence for the dead.

Ellie Maidment (11)
The Adeyfield Academy, Longlands

Soon He Will Come Home

In the name of peace we are left alone,
For with bravery they attempt to win the war,
And we wait, hoping they will return home,
And that they are not laid on a field forever cold,

His last letter feels like years ago,
I pray that the post will bring one more,
For I'll be notified if he is laid below,
Shortly he will return home...

Khaira Joosub (12)
The Adeyfield Academy, Longlands

Remembrance Monday

Every year in Adeyfield
Remembrance Day happens on the 11th of November
And on this day there are certain changes
Such as people coming wearing cadet outfits
And selling poppies for donations to charity
Also ten minutes before break the bell goes off
And we go towards the bottom court
To serve our two minutes
For all the fallen soldiers.

Kaiden Gair (13)
The Adeyfield Academy, Longlands

Freedom

They fall, while we rise
The roses grow
As we grow with them
We look around and see what the world has become
But it happened because of those who gave their lives for everyone
The men fought for our freedom
Knowing they might no longer be breathing
Their lives are gone
But we have freedom
So we should thank those and not forget.

Beau Zikmund (13)
The Adeyfield Academy, Longlands

War Horse

The Ferghana horse of the Bactrian breed,
Is short of leg but built for speed,
Ears sharp, alert, standing erect,
Its barrel chest exudes power,
And at full gallop, it will subject,
The wind to its commanding grace,
And distance disappears,
To nothingness at its great pace,
Its stamina is legendary,
And its courage will carry,
You on mythical journeys,
In just a single day.

Bobby Garrad (11)
The Adeyfield Academy, Longlands

Remember

Where the poppies grow
The men who fought are buried below
Just imagine if you remember
That's why we stand and remember
All the ones who fought are so brave
Unfortunately now they are in a grave
They must be so depressed
Certainly not calm, all stressed.

I got shot in the head
I am dead
Chilling in my death bed.

Archie Howard (13)
The Adeyfield Academy, Longlands

Peace

P eace is always needed, but not always granted.
E veryone wants peace, but others always want chaos.
A nywhere peace could reach if we let it.
C alming is what peace is, but not everyone will accept it.
E verything needs peace.

Peace is beautiful, if only the world accepted it in their time of need...

Logan Pope (12)
The Adeyfield Academy, Longlands

The Remembrance Day For Those Who Have Fallen

After both world wars, there were some who had fallen,
We celebrate Remembrance Day by doing two minutes of silence,
Someone blows a trumpet and plays a song,
They do that on Remembrance Day every day at eleven o'clock,
They do that because we need to remember those who have fallen.
And remember not to make any more mistakes and wars.

Alex Przybylski (12)
The Adeyfield Academy, Longlands

War

I close my eyes to go to sleep every night,
I try not to weep,

The war to end all wars, they said,
To those who are now horribly dead,

They say the desert dog will learn,
From its archenemy, the lion,
It seems to me that where those cities burn,
There must be mothers left in sadness,
Watching everything burn.

Lilly Juster (11)
The Adeyfield Academy, Longlands

Remembrance Day

They faked their age
Just to die
Unknowing of the danger

The red part of a poppy
Signals their blood
The leaf
Is the dead part of the ground
The black stem
Is their special hats
Covered in mud

So we wear the poppy
To show our respect
To the people
Who fought
For our freedom.

Obie Proctor Mckeown (11)
The Adeyfield Academy, Longlands

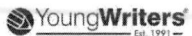

The First People In The Trenches

In the dank mud and the mist of the world's wound
You can sense dismay in the humid air
In the trenches deep where the souls lie
The bombs will fall and the rifles will continue to pour endless rounds
Bullets plummet down while the people shout with no doubt
People scream with passion and fight like their families depend on it.

Drew Campbell (11)
The Adeyfield Academy, Longlands

Remembrance Day

We stand in line, silence overtaking the school,
The whistle blows, and the trumpets start.
The respect towards the people who suffered,
Protecting and fighting for their country.
The silence for the people who have lost
Their loved ones to war, their family, friends,
Dads, sons, husbands,
The soldiers who fought in pain.

Summer Ford (14)
The Adeyfield Academy, Longlands

The Realities Of War

T iring
H orrible
E nemy

R ivalry
E ffect on the country
A ggression
L aunching things
T renches
I mpact
E nmity
S truggle

O n edge
F ighting

W arfare
A rmy
R iot.

Lylah Akram-White (12)
The Adeyfield Academy, Longlands

The Reality Of War

The guns on their backs
The fumes in the air
The shots in the distance
The dirt on my hands.

The people on the floor
The smell of sweat
The screams of my friends
The blood on my hands.

My family on the porch
The cooking in the kitchen
The music on the radio
The warmth on my fingers.

Quinn Tucker (12)
The Adeyfield Academy, Longlands

Poppies

The vermilion flowers in the wind sway,
In the sunlit fields, day after day.
Standing like guards, their red petals blow,
Poppies flow in Flanders fields as their memories glow.

Poppies remember lives that have gone,
Under the bright summer sun.
Where grenades were thrown,
Crimson flowers have grown.

Keira Merrick (12)
The Adeyfield Academy, Longlands

The Lost Pilot

Sometime this day would come,
He looked so numb.
But another one he loved,
Died in flight.

Caught him out with a serious fright,
And all peace is left,
Within this theft.
All lonely and lost in this pain,
He was never coming back to those bad raids.

Like he never left his family and friends.

Edie Lowe (12)
The Adeyfield Academy, Longlands

Poppies' Light

Life of a soldier, we won't always know
Where he lies, poppies grow
The world isn't always right
Nor are those who fight
Still, there is a light
In the way of harm's sight
Again and again
We remember the service of women and men
On this day, we remember the war
Each year and forevermore.

Nate Barringer (12)
The Adeyfield Academy, Longlands

The Poppy Field

I walk through the battleground,
Sounds of trumpets sound all around.
Gunshots stop and men fall down,
War is over, there is no need to worry now.
The guns have stilled, the smoke has cleared,
Echoes of the battle now seared.
No more the charge, the fight, the flame,
Just whispered grief that knows no name.

Yakira Peri-Taylor (12)
The Adeyfield Academy, Longlands

The 11th Of November

Remember the war
Remember the people
Remember the country
Remember the silence
Peace for the people
Remember kindness
Remember the people gone
Remember the time life would've been different
Peace for the people
Respect for the people
Kindness for the people
Silence for the people.

Jessica Speirs (14)
The Adeyfield Academy, Longlands

Gone But Never Forgotten

Guns fired mercilessly,
Boys slaughtered before they were men,
No joy, only pain and fear,
Fear that envelops the men who fight for what they love,
It is this suffering that occurred all those years ago,
Hard fought and sorely won,
It is both this victory and end to such suffering that we celebrate annually.

Mya Caseman (13)
The Adeyfield Academy, Longlands

Adeyfield On The 11th

As I was walking to school,
Everyone was wearing red poppies.
The sky was bright blue,
People were dressed in their uniforms,
For cadets and guides.

Every person in the school went to the courts,
To have two minutes of silence,
Someone was playing the trumpet.
We ended the day in peace.

Florence Lilley (11)
The Adeyfield Academy, Longlands

Pray

As a shower above
Hits the ground, or at least
I think. This war has been going
On for ages. Warm food. Playing
With my thoughts. Instead I'm
Brought to the trench again.
When will this end? Pray to
God. I might get slayed by the
Time it ends. I can't bear it
Any longer.

Michael Hitchman (11)
The Adeyfield Academy, Longlands

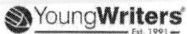

All Things I Felt

Tragedy, blood, screams, sounds, gunshots, planes up above, dropping bombs
Running, crying, yelling, shooting, crashing all things I heard
Dripping, clanking, banging, thundering of tanks, footsteps, swooshing, roaring all things I heard
Tragedy, blood, screams, gunshots, running, yelling, all things I felt.

Alex Curtis-whittaker (11)
The Adeyfield Academy, Longlands

The Little Boy At War

A little boy tall and slim,
Sat down ready for his trim.

The little boy put on his boots and told to march,
The little boy leaving home for a camp very large.

A little boy looking at death,
Stopping for a second and smelling his breath,
A little boy headed home and told to rest.

Amber Wiley (13)
The Adeyfield Academy, Longlands

The Warriors Of War

Sadness of war
The hope for peace
Soldiers coming and going
The constant worry of being shot
I thought it would be a month or two
But it's turning into years

Boom! Crashing of bombs
Gas rolling in
Never-ending noise
Will it ever end?
I hope so.

Oliver Wharfe (11)
The Adeyfield Academy, Longlands

Poppies

Poppies are colourful soldiers who died
Poppies grew on the battlefields
Yet it's not a colourful place
Brave men fought
Yet they get nothing in return
And just get forgotten
The only thing that makes them get remembered
Are the poppies that grew on their graves.

Ollie Jones (12)
The Adeyfield Academy, Longlands

The Day Of Remembrance

Years ago in 1918,
on the eleventh month,
on the eleventh day,
on the eleventh hour,
the tragic war that was World War One ended.
Millions of men,
day and night,
sacrificed their lives for their country.
They lived in the trenches filled with rats and dirt.

Joshua Ball (12)
The Adeyfield Academy, Longlands

Goodbye My Fellow Friends

Boys lined up in uniform hoping they
would see this wonderful place again.
Girls underground clinging,
crying hoping it would just stop.
Men's names etched on plaques
as they closed their weary eyes.
Their souls in poppy fields
as we say our goodbyes.

Jessica Renyard (11)
The Adeyfield Academy, Longlands

Peace

Hope for peace
How it's rare
We hope for kindness
But kindness is not there
Some believe and some do not
Some have kindness and some have none
The war is sad
And those who died
Will be remembered
And their souls will thrive.

Maddie Smith (13)
The Adeyfield Academy, Longlands

The Last Goodbye

Dear my wonderful family
I am writing this to say
you will be okay
though I am gone
you must be strong
a single poppy will mark my rest
wear that poppy in remembrance
though I shall always be with you
I must leave you
goodbye.

Sophia Ward (11)
The Adeyfield Academy, Longlands

War Poem

Where the poppies now grow
I was fighting a long time ago
I was shooting someone with a weapon
Now I wish that didn't happen

I was shooting someone with good aim
And then I did it again
I once was screaming
Now I am dreaming.

Edward Matei (12)
The Adeyfield Academy, Longlands

Untitled

People fleeing to shelter
Crying, hoping it would stop
Young men sacrificing
Themselves for their country
Their names etched on plaques lined up
As they close their weary eyes
As we look over the poppy fields
We remember the loss.

Jessica Renyard (11)
The Adeyfield Academy, Longlands

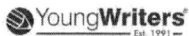

The Final Thoughts

He was hit and he lies,
All he can think is how has his life ended like this?
From an unknown combatant he has never seen, he lies,
Thinking about family and friends, some he has lost.
Gunfire rings out all around him, but all he can do is lie.

Charlie Wharfe (14)
The Adeyfield Academy, Longlands

Remembrance

People wear poppies from the start of November,
As a way for those lost to remain remembered.
They symbolise the death, the blood, but new life,
After soldiers went through years of strife.
Some people dismiss as though they don't care.

Cassidy Farkas (12)
The Adeyfield Academy, Longlands

Remember

We remember the 11th of November
The day the poppies grew
When the soldiers lost a shoe
When the bomb that they threw
Went boom
Now we wear the
Poppies because they bloom
To show who we remember
On the 11th of November.

Lucie Evans (13)
The Adeyfield Academy, Longlands

In The Fields Of War

In the fields of war,
The poppies blow between the crosses,
Row on row.
That marks the place on the ground.

And in the skies,
Not days ago,
We lived, and saw the sun glow.
We are the dead,
Who forever grow.

Riley Summerfield (11)
The Adeyfield Academy, Longlands

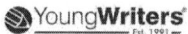

The Grief Of War

Saddened by the death of men
The sacrifice they had given
May they rest in heaven
The innocence of children
The vehicles in green
Of which had stolen
Many precious living moments
Taken...
With no mercy upon.

Rahil Khan (11)
The Adeyfield Academy, Longlands

Poppies Bloom

In the fields the poppies bloom,
Those young men gone too soon.
Their dreams shattered, their bodies lie still,
Now becoming one with the ground.
Bound to their eternal sleep,
The wives of those men start to weep.

Lucas Butler (12)
The Adeyfield Academy, Longlands

The Place They Stay

Where the poppies were laid,
That's where they stay,
People lay,
They get visited every day,
How many times a day?
They may not stay,
Where the poppies were laid,

That's where they stay.

Oscar Harris (12)
The Adeyfield Academy, Longlands

The Price Of Peace

Beneath
the broken sky,
the silence speaks of the broken men who had never returned.
In rusted fields, their names still wait. The voice of the fallen calls in the wind
although their lips have been long sealed.

Mateo Jalba (12)
The Adeyfield Academy, Longlands

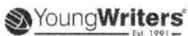

Poppies

When you go out to fight,
You put yourself to fight for our country.
But the government also should put themselves out there.
But they don't, so it's very sad,
But that is the world we live in.

Malakai Hamidy (12)
The Adeyfield Academy, Longlands

The Sad War

We gather here today
with a sorrowful heart
full of tears
with a soft heart.
We shall stand in silence
and remember our soldiers.
Till the day we die
they shall stay in our hearts.

Abbas Juma (13)
The Adeyfield Academy, Longlands

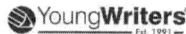

Remembrance Day

As we step into school
We get greeted by people
Holding boxes of poppies
To remember this day
For all the people we lost today
Hoping that they see us
Celebrating their special day.

Chloe Carter (13) & Ellie-Marie
The Adeyfield Academy, Longlands

Poppy, Poppy

Poppy, poppy, what do you say?
Wear me on Remembrance Day
Poppy, poppy, what do you tell?
Many soldiers in battle fell
Poppy, poppy, what should we know?
That peace on Earth should grow.

Jack Gransden (12)
The Adeyfield Academy, Longlands

Battle Cry

Running through the battlefield
Waiting for the bang
As metal swords near me go clang
Everyone I love flashes before my eyes
As I hope I won't die
Seeing my friend slowly die
I pick him up as I cry.

Evie Thomas (11)
The Adeyfield Academy, Longlands

Wars End

Wake up, it's time for war,
All men, even the poor

That morning alarm,
the worst possible sound,
Yet the beds as hard as metal
that weighs one hundred times a pound.

Frankie Harthill (11)
The Adeyfield Academy, Longlands

The Sadness Of War

The strokes of a drum call, the horns arise
A distant cry beneath the skies
With hearts of steel, we march in line
To face the war, divine
The earth is torn, the skies are red.

Haris Khan (14)
The Adeyfield Academy, Longlands

The Innocence Of Children

Once they played in fields of green,
Dreamed of what to be.
Laughter echoed, jokes were told,
Thought to do the same tomorrow.
The sky was black,
Shots were fired.

Grace Wells (12)
The Adeyfield Academy, Longlands

Dear Diary

Dear Diary,
Tonight I heard the bombs soaring through the air,
And crashing beneath me,
I could smell smoke rising up,
Running,
Screaming,
Silence.

Kaitlyn Johnson (11)
The Adeyfield Academy, Longlands

I Saw

I saw bravery
I saw loyalty in a young man
I saw a scared young boy wanting to be held by his mum
I saw my mate being blown up
I saw blood of my own.

Katie Southam (13)
The Adeyfield Academy, Longlands

War Is...

War
Is a waste of resources
Is a waste of life
Is a waste of humanity
Is a waste of time
War is a bleeding wound
We need to save our time.

Lily-Grace Wingrove (14)
The Adeyfield Academy, Longlands

The Soldiers Who Risked Their Lives

The soldiers who risked their lives
Will be hearts for the rest of our lives
The war killed many
They really tried.
People in tears.

Gurneet Kaur (11)
The Adeyfield Academy, Longlands

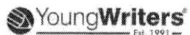

Remembering The Soldiers

Murky depths of shallow ground,
Remembering the brave soldiers not long ago,
Poppies grow tall and proud,
Swaying in the wind.

Hollie (11)
The Adeyfield Academy, Longlands

Untitled

The sadness of soldiers,
The beauty of peace,
War is pain but this must cease,
The poppies stain among the soldiers.

Maryam Iqbal (11)
The Adeyfield Academy, Longlands

Cry For Help

The darkness is upon them,
Sirens blaring - the war has begun.
This marks the beginning of the mayhem,
As war roared on, soldiers started to make a plan.
Explosive fumes fill the fogged air,
The burning flesh smelt from far and wide.
The immense pressure the soldiers had to bear,
There was nothing left but their pride.
All that is left is a sea of motionless bodies.
As the sun rises, poppies grow,
A beautiful sight after such a tragic event.
The eerie silence compared to such screams.

Lana Gidlow (12)
The West Grantham CE Secondary Academy, Grantham

World War

Opposition tanks rattling across the floor,
Many people freezing cold.
I cry while looking at my best friend,
Torn to shreds,
Body parts flying everywhere.

The world being destroyed as I blink,
Poisonous bombs killing my insides.
I hate this war,
I wish it would just stop and end.
This war is ruining the world.

Hope Howkins (13)
The West Grantham CE Secondary Academy, Grantham

We Will Remember

You gave your lives,
For us to live.
We will remember,
What you did.

The poppy is a symbol,
Of the sacrifice you made.
We wear it with pride,
We know you were afraid.

You bravely fought,
For the freedom we have today.
You gave us a pathway,
Rest in peace where you lie.

Wear your poppy to remember,
Every day throughout November.
Because the lessons we have learnt,
Must never be forgotten.

Dylan Wilkins (10)
Ysgol Gynradd Gymunedol Gymraeg Llantrisant, Miskin

Young Writers Information

We hope you have enjoyed reading this book – and that you will continue to in the coming years.

If you're the parent or family member of an enthusiastic poet or story writer, do visit our website **www.youngwriters.co.uk/subscribe** and sign up to receive news, competitions, writing challenges and tips, activities and much, much more! There's lots to keep budding writers motivated!

If you would like to order further copies of this book, or any of our other titles, then please give us a call or order via your online account.

Young Writers
Remus House
Coltsfoot Drive
Peterborough
PE2 9BF
(01733) 890066
info@youngwriters.co.uk

Join in the conversation!
Tips, news, giveaways and much more!

YoungWritersUK   YoungWritersCW
youngwriterscw   youngwriterscw